DATE DUE	
DEC 3 1991	
JAN 2 9 1992	
FEB 8 1992	
FEB 8 1992	
FEB 2 1993	
ILL 6-25-93	
MAR. 4 1994	
ILL 9-15-94	
FEB 21 1995	
FEB 2 8 1996	
JUN 2 7 1996	
OCT 25 1996	
ILL 10-15-97	
JAN 0 9 1998	

MAJOLICA

MAJOLICA

Nicholas M. Dawes

Crown Publishers, Inc.
New York

Designed by Nancy Kenmore
Line art ornaments by
Jennifer Harper
Copyright © 1990 by Nicholas M. Dawes

Published by Crown Publishers, Inc., 201 East 50th Street
New York, New York 10022

CROWN is a trademark of Crown Publishers, Inc.

Manufactured in Japan

Library of Congress Cataloging-in-Publication Data

Dawes, Nicholas M.
Majolica

Includes bibliographical references (p. 187) and index.
1. Majolica, English.   2. Majolica—19th century—England
3. Majolica, American.   4. Majolica—19th century—United
States.   I. Title.
NK4320.G7D38   1990   738.3'7   90–2487
ISBN 0-517-57757-7
10   9   8   7   6   5   4   3   2   1
First Edition

For
my
mother

C o n t e n t s

I owe my fascination with ceramics largely to my parents and am greatly indebted to them for it, as I am for many things. Some of my earliest memories are of my father returning home late from night school in Stoke-on-Trent, where he learned the rudiments of technique from which he later built a career around the ceramics industry. This included a period of employment as kiln foreman in a brickworks, where I regularly "helped" him check kiln temperatures as a young boy. During adolescence, I learned to identify and value English ceramics from my mother, whose pursuit of antiques dealings brought her into close contact with two centuries of Staffordshire wares.

The Potteries of North Staffordshire are more than an ocean from New York City, however, and I am grateful to Lisa Healy, Senior Editor and Special Projects Editor at Crown Publishers, for her professional insight and for rekindling my own interest in this subject with such enthusiasm.

I extend sincere gratitude to those collectors who generously shared their homes, collections, and knowledge of majolica with me, especially Dr. and Mrs. Howard Silby, Gerry and Aviva Leberfeld, and Mrs. Stuart Kadison, all of whom have contributed generously and invaluably to this book.

I also thank other collectors who have supplied illustrations, namely Joan Esch, Denny and Elaine Lotwin, Lloyd J. Bleier, and Mr. and Mrs. I. Chisholm, and I extend a special thanks to Rita and Ian Smythe of Britannia Antiques in London, whose

e d g m e n t s

stall in Gray's Market is a justifiably well-known hub of majolica activity for collectors and trade alike.

I am indebted to Joan Jones, curator, and her excellent staff at the Minton Museum (Royal Doulton Tableware Ltd.), in Stoke-on-Trent for their enthusiastic and professional support. Similarly, I thank Gaye Blake Roberts, Lynn Miller, and the Trustees of the Wedgwood Museum in Barlaston. I also thank the staff of the City Museum and Art Gallery in Stoke-on-Trent, the Gladstone Pottery Museum in Longton, the Hanley Reference Library and the Ironbridge Gorge Museum in Shropshire, as well as the Chester County Historical Society in Pennsylvania, and the Cooper Hewitt Museum Library in New York City.

I am grateful to J. Garvin Mecking, whom I was privileged to know before his premature death in 1989, and his staff in New York, Mr. Dwight Crockett in particular. I also thank the representatives of The Haldon Group, Mottahedeh and Porta, who supplied information and illustrations used in chapter 7.

I gratefully acknowledge the research assistance from Susan Pennington and the extensive general assistance from Julie Pottak. I extend a warm thanks to Sara Lee Adams for her dedication in typing the manuscript and a special appreciation to Terry McGinniss, the New York photographer, for his excellent contributions.

Finally, I thank my wife, Rosemarie, for her support and enthusiasm.

Y ou who in these parts
make such hard,
smooth, well-compacted,
and enduring pottery understand
well that you must give it
other qualities besides those which
make it fit for ordinary use.
You must profess to make it beautiful
as well as useful, and if you
did not you would certainly
lose your market. That has been the
view the world has taken of
your art, and of all the industrial arts
since the beginning of history.

William Morris,
from an address to the people
of Burslem,
October 13, 1881

I ~ n ~ t ~ r ~ o ~ d

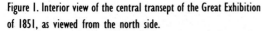

Figure 1. Interior view of the central transept of the Great Exhibition of 1851, as viewed from the north side.

A remarkable testament to the powers behind the Crystal Palace Exhibition of 1851 is that it is still popularly known as the "Great Exhibition." Hyde Park, in the center of Victorian London, was the ideal setting for an exhibition of such magnitude and prospect, featuring one enormous iron-framed building, designed by Joseph Paxton, overflowing with new products and ideas from all corners of the globe in a celebration of decorative and industrial arts of unprecedented scale. Credit for the organization of the exhibition has traditionally been attributed to Prince Albert, husband of Queen Victoria, acting in his nominal role as promoter of British commercial interests and also as president of the Fine Arts Commission, and to Sir Henry Cole (1802–1882), the industrial designer.

Cole was among those singular members of early Victorian English society who dedicated themselves to the promotion of industrial arts, a respectable social pursuit at that time, which, alas, has fallen from favor. In a letter written several years after the exhibition,[1] Cole himself attributed the exhibition's conception on an international scale and its subsequent success to Herbert Minton (1793–1858), the distinguished potter whom he had befriended in the late 1840s. Minton's display was prominent among the English contribution, and he chose the exhibition forum to introduce a number of "new lines," notably a strikingly polychromatic and lustrous glazed earthenware of Renaissance inspiration termed "Majolica."

Herbert Minton began potting for his father at the age of thirteen and, by 1851, was the successful owner of four large factories in Stoke-on-Trent employing over 1,000 workers.[2] Blessed with the provincial enlightenment of such luminaries as Josiah Wedgwood I, Minton recognized London as the capital of a vast and expanding empire and the Great Exhibition as an event of unprecedented international importance, which, as his nephew, Colin Minton Campbell, observed, could determine the "super excellence of any one person."[3] Herbert Minton retired four years after the Great Exhibition to the South Coast of England, where he died three years later, but the majolica ware he had introduced in 1851 continued to bring prosperity to the company for the rest of the century, fulfilling his personal aspirations and the Great Exhibition's commercial promise.

Minton's success in 1851 was not shared by all the British contingent, how-

ever. Henry Cole and his followers vociferously criticized the mainstream ornamental taste on display, condemning it as inferior and evidence of the failure of the Art Reform movement to unite art and industry effectively or produce new and progressive design concepts. The main thrust of Cole's criticism was toward the overwhelming use of historic revivalism in popular design, much of which was of incongruous or poorly conceived application. It is unfortunate that all Victorian Revivalist styles still suffer from the stigma of the Great Exhibition's post mortem and are commonly considered to be deficient in design merit. While it is true that the banner of revivalism afforded respectability to all interpretations or facsimiles of historical styles, many talented and progressive individuals worked cleverly within the movement.

This distinction between designers who exploit historicism and those who understand and interpret it was recognized by Henry Cole, who personally encouraged "progressive revivalism" under his pseudonym Felix Summerly[4] and practiced by Minton, who presented majolica ware as evidence of his understanding of contemporary positivist art theory as applied to ceramics:

> The revival or imitation, when not carried too far, of any of the historic styles of pottery is always to be commended; in as much as it brings modern methods and skills face to face with the past.[5]

No individual pursued the objective to "bring modern methods and skills face to face with the past" more earnestly than Joseph François Leon Arnoux (1816–1902), designer of the Minton stand at the Great Exhibition who successfully met the challenge of tastefully reproducing Renaissance ceramics with the majolica he invented. Arnoux was born into a distinguished family of potters from Toulouse and was sufficiently qualified, when he visited Stoke-on-Trent in 1848, for Herbert Minton to offer him the prestigious position of art director; he accepted, bringing his young West Indian wife and child to the Potteries. Arnoux's academic training[6] and remarkable knowledge of traditional French potting made him uniquely qualified to pursue the "lost arts" practiced by Renaissance potters on a Victorian commercial scale, demand for which was generated by an emerging affluent class who looked to the future for inspiration and to the past, including sixteenth-century Italy, for parallels of wealth and power. Further-

Figure 2. Herbert Minton, from a portrait by H. W. Pickersgill, R. A. Minton recognized the importance of the Great Exhibition, and his influence with Henry Cole helped shape its scale and subsequent success.

more, public awareness and respect for Renaissance ceramics was increased through the publication of several illustrated works on the subject[7] and the establishment of public museums, which by mid-century had placed private collections on display for the first time.[8]

Such displays inspired Arnoux and his contemporaries to imitate historic objects to an authentic result (Figure 3), in much the same manner that glass from the ancient world inspired "Art Glass" manufacturers a quarter of a century later. Arnoux's majolica was undoubtedly the most successful of these historically based ventures, which included the production of Henri-Deux ware[9] by Minton with technically magnificent but commercially disappointing results.

Ironically, majolica's commercial success and longevity was achieved by deviating, almost immediately, from historical authenticity to meet popular demand. Thus,

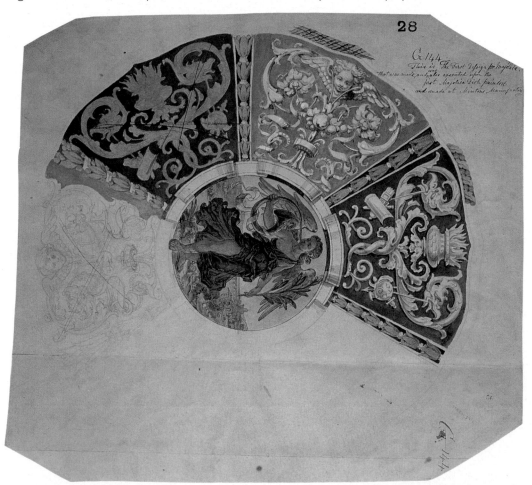

Figure 3. Design for a plate to be painted in majolica colors in imitation of sixteenth-century Italian *maiolica* by Thomas Kirkby, 1850. The majolica glazes formulated by Leon Arnoux during his early years at Minton were used on a range of authentic reproductions of Renaissance ceramics, mostly copied by Thomas Kirkby, as well as conventional majolica in contemporary taste. *Minton Museum, Royal Doulton Ltd.*

Figure 4. Minton majolica flower vase, date code for 1851, height 7". Some early examples of Minton majolica are small in scale and finely modeled, comparable to contemporary porcelain made to adorn the mantelpieces of fashionable houses in the 1850s. *Collection of Dr. & Mrs. Howard Silby*

Figure 5. Design drawing for majolica ice stand, circa 1851 (majolica design number 42), from the Minton majolica rag books. More ornamental than functional, ice stands were among the earliest specialized ware in contemporary taste produced in Minton majolica. *Minton Museum, Royal Doulton Ltd.*

Figure 6. Minton majolica cachepôt, *opposite*, designed circa 1851, supported by four terminal bacchanalian figures, each wall painted with a circular seascape panel, possibly by Edward Rischgitz, date code for 1864, height 9½". Much of Minton's early majolica ware included painted panels. This model was exhibited in Paris in 1855 and may have been included in the Great Exhibition. *Britannia, Gray's Antique Market, London*

the earliest examples of majolica, designed at Minton by Arnoux, often in collaboration with Thomas Kirkby, his principal designer at the time, are representations and, in some cases, facsimiles of Italian Renaissance ceramics, sometimes including overglaze, enamel-painted ornament. Ware of this type continued in production at Minton until the 1860s, when a few examples were also made by Wedgwood, but represents a tiny proportion of the ware that can be classified as "English majolica," the vast majority of which consists of "modern" forms decorated in the range of opaque "majolica" glazes developed by Arnoux before 1851 (Figures 4 and 5).

This distinction between historically authentic, Renaissance-inspired ware and Arnoux's lustrous glazed majolica first caused confusion at the Great Exhibition, when art critics referred to the new line under a variety of terms, including "*cinque-cento* ware" and "English Maiolica," despite Minton's advertisement of it all as simply, "majolica." The word is, therefore, a trade name, introduced as early as 1849, when it first appears in Minton's pattern books,[10] and has remained the subject of much confusion ever since. It is derived, for prestigious reasons, from *maiolica*, the Italian word for tin-glazed earthenware, which itself is a corrupt form of Majorca, the Mediterranean island through which tin-glazed earthenware was imported from North Africa and the Near East into Italy during the Renaissance.

Technically, English majolica as devised by Leon Arnoux most closely resembles the characteristic, polychromatic earthenwares first made in Florence by a process commonly attributed to Luca della Robbia (1400–1482).[11] Robbia and his followers, including his nephew Andrea (1435–1528) made a calcareous, biscuit-fired body painted in part with opaque, colored glazes and enamels that replaced the conventional coating of opaque white (tin) glaze upon which enamel colors and coatings of clear glaze could be added (Figure 8). Robbia's process was ideally suited to the production of sculptural ware, and typical examples include plaques and architectural ornament modeled in high relief after designs by prominent contemporary artists, including Brunelleschi.

It is important to remember that English majolica, along with its Continental and American versions, is a Victorian ceramic invention and not directly evolved from Renaissance or other *maiolica*. Even the few early examples previously mentioned are no more than visual reproductions of earlier *maiolica* and were not made in the tin-glazed earthenware technique.

Figure 7. Majolica-glazed relief portrait tile of the Right Honorable William Ewart Gladstone (1809–1898), who served as British Prime Minister between 1868 and 1894 and publicly supported the politics of Reform. *Ironbridge Gorge Museum Trust*

Thus, the connection between *maiolica* and majolica is mainly an etymological one; the former term applies to a particular earthenware type, while the latter describes a characteristic form of glazing (any) ceramic body. The word can also be used adjectivally (as in "majolica glazes") and is more precise when given one of several preceding modifiers, including "industrial"—many products with majolica glaze were sold as "industrial majolica" in the nineteenth century—or a modifier denoting origin, such as "English," "Continental" or "American," all of which imply a variation on the technique.

As a prominent collector recently remarked, "If only they had called it 'Arnoux ware,' we would have been spared the confusion."

Figure 8. A relief panel in polychromed terra cotta from the workshop of Andrea della Robbia, circa 1600, diameter 3'3". The advanced ceramics of Luca della Robbia and his followers provided technical and artistic inspiration to Victorian majolica manufacturers.

English Majolica:
The Birth of an Industry

The Politics of Majolica: Reform and Revolution

The story of English majolica is confined to the middle years of the reign of Queen Victoria, roughly 1850 to 1890, with production peaking in output and demand around 1875. Despite the relatively short period of production, English majolica made a global impact on taste, which was all but relegated to obscurity by contemporary changes in demand and ambivalence by twentieth-century scholars toward later nineteenth-century decorative arts. In recent years, English majolica has enjoyed a considerable revival in popularity, evident in soaring prices for better examples in the marketplace, new scholarship, and a profusion of modern reproductions. The genesis of majolica in the Staffordshire potteries resulted from a coincidence of political, scientific, and artistic events and trends.

Two distinct developments in mid-nineteenth-century European politics contributed directly to the development of English majolica: the Reform movement in Britain, which spurned the products we term "architectural majolica," and the Paris Revolution of 1848, which helped establish North Staffordshire as the international center of majolica production.

The second quarter of the nineteenth century was a period of intense governmental reform in Great Britain at national and local levels. Parliamentarians, industrialists, clergy, gentry, trade unionists, and philanthropists of all callings strove to improve the nation's electoral system, infrastructure, and working conditions, especially in the rapidly expanding urban industrial areas that included the Potteries. Among the most worthwhile achievements of this movement were the abolition of slavery in the West Indies, the control of child labor, and the introduction of legislation to improve standards of sanitation. This latter development was

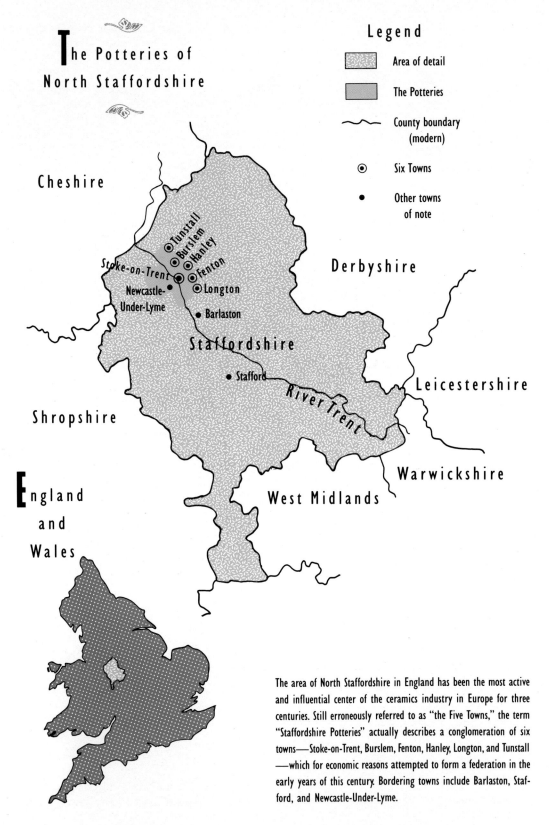

The Potteries of North Staffordshire

Legend

▨ Area of detail

▨ The Potteries

〰 County boundary (modern)

◉ Six Towns

● Other towns of note

Cheshire

Tunstall
Burslem
Hanley
Stoke-on-Trent
Fenton
Newcastle-Under-Lyme
Longton
Barlaston

Derbyshire

Staffordshire

River Trent

Stafford

Leicestershire

Shropshire

Warwickshire

England and Wales

West Midlands

The area of North Staffordshire in England has been the most active and influential center of the ceramics industry in Europe for three centuries. Still erroneously referred to as "the Five Towns," the term "Staffordshire Potteries" actually describes a conglomeration of six towns—Stoke-on-Trent, Burslem, Fenton, Hanley, Longton, and Tunstall—which for economic reasons attempted to form a federation in the early years of this century. Bordering towns include Barlaston, Stafford, and Newcastle-Under-Lyme.

prompted by the deplorable conditions of public health in early Victorian England, which had resulted in outbreaks of deadly cholera in epidemic proportions. The governmental responsibility for alleviating these conditions rested with the Poor Law Commissions, which were headed by Edwin Chadwick during the most intense period of reform in the 1840s. Chadwick's *Report on the Sanitary Conditions of the Labouring Population*, published in 1842, popularized the belief that cholera and similar diseases were directly related to contaminated water supply, a phenomenon that was still widely unrecognized at the time. By the mid-1850s, Chadwick's theory had been medically proven, and his solutions—the safe treatment of sewage and a durable underground sewer system with separate, piped, pure water—precipitated a new British ceramic industry. From simple salt-glazed sewer pipes to magnificent glazed tiling and architectural faience, the early design and manufacturing of sanitary ware in all forms has provided us with a legacy of unique Victorian ceramic art.

The name of Doulton is most closely associated with the development of this type of ware. Founded by John Doulton in 1815 with an investment of one hundred pounds, the modern company, known as Royal Doulton Tableware Ltd., is one of the largest producers of decorative and industrial ceramics in the world and owner of Minton and other trade names. Doulton began operating in Lambeth in South London and, after 1877, expanded to Burslem, Staffordshire, as the company flourished on an unprecedented scale throughout the last half of the nineteenth century. This success was largely due to their concentration on developing a reputation as manufacturers of sanitary drain pipes, demand for which was especially felt in London. Indeed, according to Paul Atterbury and Louise Irvine, authors of *The Doulton Story*, "without the drains there would have been no Doulton story to tell."[1] During the 1850s and early 1860s, Doulton's successes and huge demands encouraged many established potters to enter the new field of production and created a host of specialist manufacturers.

The highly competitive nature of the industry, coupled with the enormous quantities of materials required at a time of seemingly limitless expansion, forced manufacturers to keep production costs at a minimum. Thus, salt glazing, an inexpensive technique requiring the introduction of common rock salt to the kiln at a critical point in the firing process, was favored, especially by Doulton's, which had pioneered the technique, and unglazed terra cotta architectural ornament of red or buff coloration was the material of choice for other manufacturers. By the mid-1860s, the general availability of opaque majolica glazes, coupled with contemporary advancements in such areas of production as tile pressing and glost kilns, made the manufacture of glazed architectural ceramics economically viable. Production was encouraged by demands from a public fascinated by the advanced ceramics of Renaissance Europe, especially the colorful, tin-glazed architectural ornament of Luca della Robbia and his followers, and by increasing pressure from progressive architects and public health reformers for exterior surfaces of city buildings that were not only easy to clean but that would resist an atmosphere thick with the polluting filth of Victorian heavy industry as well as the abuse from British weather. Halsey Ricardo, the socialite architect who designed majolica-tiled fireplace mantels in collaboration with Wedgwood,[2] was a protagonist in this cause, arguing "red brick and terra cotta discolor, colored stones and marbles grow dim and perish in shocking haste; and it would seem as if no building material but what had got practically a glass face to it would be able to contend against the corrosion of the air of a manufacturing town."[3]

Ricardo's arguments were well founded, and by the end of the century, ceramic surfaces with majolica, clear or salt glazes unsurped virtually all

Figure 10. Terra-cotta roundel of "Autumn" from a series of the Four Seasons by Maw & Company, circa 1860, diameter 12". The demand for ornamental terra cotta for architectural purposes was met by a number of manufacturers by the middle of the nineteenth century. The ware is relatively easy to manufacture in unglazed state. *Ironbridge Gorge Museum Trust*

other types of building materials as they became less expensive and their qualities became justly recognized.

Doulton made little decorative ware that can be accurately termed "English majolica." In the 1870s, the firm concentrated on the production of "Doultonware," a dense, highly resistant salt-glazed stoneware, for exterior use but also produced majolica-glazed tiles and some faience of the highest order that was shipped to commissions around the world. The durability and suitability for purpose of Doulton's architectural ware is evidenced by the many fine examples that still exist, including the magnificent interior of Harrod's food halls in London, completed in 1905.

Minton was among the earliest manufacturers to succeed in commercial production of glazed

architectural ceramics, a fine example of which is preserved *in situ* in the Gamble Room at the Victoria & Albert Museum. Formerly the central of three refreshment rooms installed in the museum under the guidance of its original director, Sir Henry Cole, the Gamble Room was completed in 1867 and is named for James Gamble, the principal designer of the tiling therein. Majolica tiling was selected partly for its sanitary value, and the room features four majolica-clad iron columns that support the vaulted ceiling. Credit for the early application of majolica glazes onto terra cotta can also be given to Maw & Company, which also contributed tiling for the Gamble Room project.[4] Maw was England's most successful manufacturer of glazed architectural ornament in the last half of the nineteenth century (Figures 10–13).

Figure 11. Maw & Company majolica-glazed fireplace and hearth, circa 1875. By the 1870s, a number of manufacturers, including Maw & Company, Minton, and Doulton, began applying majolica glazes to forms first made in terra cotta (in the manner of della Robbia) in response to contemporary demands from architects. *Ironbridge Gorge Museum Trust*

The company was founded by George Maw, a wealthy sophisticate and accomplished botanist, and his younger brother, Arthur, who took over an antiquated factory at Broseley on the banks of the River Severn in Shropshire to manufacture terra cotta and encaustic floor tiles, in the medieval manner, using a patent for the technique obtained from Herbert Minton. By 1883, the company had built an impressive modern factory at nearby Jackfield for the production of decorative tiling and related wares. It was the largest works of its type in the world, capable of producing over 20 million items a year.[5] By the mid-1860s, George Maw was experimenting with majolica glazes, and within a few years he introduced majolica tiles and glazed architectural ornament of a wide variety.[6] By the mid-1880s, Maw's offered an enormous range of products—over 9,000 designs in all—including ten distinctly different kinds of decorated tile that were widely recognized as being of superior design and execution (Figures 14, 15, and 16). Maw & Company maintained high standards of design by employing such prominent artists and designers as Walter Crane, who also designed "art pottery" for the works, and Lewis F. Day, along with its permanent design staff.

Other important manufacturers of architectural majolica outside Staffordshire included Craven Dunhill & Company (1871–1951), which operated from a works adjacent to Maw's in Jackfield; Carter and Company (1873–1964), located in the clay-rich town of Poole, in Dorset; and Burmantofts Faience (1882–1904) of Leeds, in Yorkshire, which also made art pottery. Within the Potteries, Minton, which also produced tiles under the name Campbell Brick & Tile Company and Minton Hollins & Company; Wedgwood; and Copeland & Sons were all prolific manufacturers of architectural majolica. George Jones did not compete in this market, although a small range of majolica tiles in six- and eight-inch square sizes were offered in the late 1870s. Specialized man-

Figure 12. Page from a Maw & Company catalog of circa 1883, *above*, illustrating part of the company's range of architectural majolica, offered as "enameled terra cotta," including the full series of Season roundels. *Ironbridge Gorge Museum Trust*

Figure 13. Elaborate majolica wall tiling, *right*, by Maw & Company in the Valley Hotel, Ironbridge, England. The Valley Hotel was formerly known as Severn House and was the residence of Arthur Maw in the 1880s, when the tiling was installed. *Ironbridge Gorge Museum Trust*

Figure 14. Maw & Company heavily molded majolica-glazed tile, *above*, with repeating motif, suitable for interior or exterior setting, circa 1885, 6″ × 6″. *Ironbridge Gorge Museum Trust*

Figure 15. Maw & Company majolica-glazed architectural panel, *below*, of a repeating frieze pattern, circa 1885, 12″ × 12″. *Ironbridge Gorge Museum Trust*

Figure 17. The bar of the Crown Liquor Saloon, *above*, Great Victoria Street, Belfast, Ireland, circa 1900. A magnificent example of the application of Victorian tiled surfaces, including extensive use of majolica-glazed tiling and faience. The scheme was designed in 1886 by Patrick Flanagan, son of the saloon's owner, and completed ten years later. All tiling is by Craven Dunhill & Company of Jackfield. *Ironbridge Gorge Museum Trust*

Figure 16. Majolica tiles, with panel suggestions, *opposite*, from a Maw & Company catalog, circa 1885. *Ironbridge Gorge Museum Trust*

Figure 18. Majolica-glazed tile and faience bar front, by Craven Dunhill & Company, at the Red Lion public house, Erdington, Birmingham, circa 1890. The combination of sanitary function and ornamental appeal made this type of majolica ware uniquely suitable for use in Victorian public houses. *Ironbridge Gorge Museum Trust*

ufacturers of note include Sherwin and Cotton of Hanley (1877–1911); T & R Boote of Burslem, which was established in 1842 and, according to one account, was "probably responsible for more majolica tiles than any other manufacturer at the turn of the century"[7]; and Malkin, Edge & Company of Burslem (1866–1968).

Throughout the last half of the nineteenth century, manufacturers of architectural majolica toiled to keep up the supply demanded by a building boom of unprecedented proportions. A cultural revolution brought millions to the cities, and a modern infrastructure of roads and railways was built to service the economy of mass consumption. Expansion was not limited to Great Britain. By 1880, Maw & Company had agents in Europe, Canada, the United States, South Africa, Australia, New Zealand, India, China, and Japan.

A combination of civic pride and civil engineering provided a marketplace for architectural majolica in public and commercial buildings of all types, especially town halls, museums, banks, and even prisons. Demands from the Public Health Acts led to the building of hospitals and pumping stations, while the new urban population enjoyed architectural majolica in the entrance halls, porticos, and fireplaces of their homes, as well as in their places of worship and entertainment. Gin palaces, practically none of which exist intact today, and public houses were especially suited to decoration with lavishly ornamental glazed surfaces (Figures 18, 19, and 20). The Victorian urban building boom was largely governed by the extent and direction of Britain's remarkable network of railways, including the underground systems that appeared in major European and American cities by the turn of the century, providing an enormous market for plain glazed tile,[8] while the stations and terminals were typically designed to incorporate architectural majolica. Owing to the incidence of private railway companies in Victorian Britain, important cities frequently featured sev-

Figure 19. View of the interior of the Crown Liquor Saloon, Great Victoria Street, Belfast, Ireland, circa 1900. *Ironbridge Gorge Museum Trust*

eral railway terminals competing with each other in the use of architectural ornament (Figures 21 and 22).

The policies of reform had a catalytic effect upon the course of British design, which affected majolica production beyond the development of architectural ware. While the Poor Law Commissioners strove to improve the nation's sanitary infrastructure, a select Parliamentary Committee was established to determine "the best means of extending knowledge of the Arts and of the Principles of Design among the [manufacturing] People," in order to improve foreign trade. Its first report, published in 1836, urged the establishment of National Schools of Design to be administered

under Government auspices, over twenty of which were in operation before the Great Exhibition (Figure 23).

This remarkable attempt by a government to infuse principles of taste into a manufacturing nation generated considerable criticism from those progressive designers who considered the schools' collective technique of preaching academic standards as contrary to the objective of uniting art and industry. Despite these shortcomings, however, the schools of design set a precedent that was widely adopted by private enterprise. The School of Design at Stoke-on-Trent, which continues operation today, was built in the early 1850s under the advice of Leon Arnoux and with finan-

MAW & COMPANY LIMITED, Benthall Works, Jackfield, Shropshire. ENGLAND.

PLATE I

Window Frame

Door Frame

Exterior Decoration
—in Constructional Faience.
Scale I″— One Foot.

Front Elevation

Sectional Elevation.

cial assistance from Herbert Minton, in whose honor it was named following his death in 1858. Many painters and modelers of English majolica learned their craft there under the tutorship of local professionals,[9] fulfilling Herbert Minton's prediction that the School "... will enable us to produce much finer works of art than we have hitherto done."[10] Prominent designers also lectured at the Coalbrookdale School of Art, in Shropshire, which was established in 1846 by the local cast-iron manufacturer to improve standards of design for castings and proved an excellent resource for the local decorative ceramics industry, notably Maw & Company and Craven Dunhill & Company (Figure 23). While the success of architectural majolica was due, in part, to far-reaching English statutes, the evolution of other majolica in England was guided by political circumstances in neighboring France.

Between 1848 and 1850, French industry and commerce crossed the English Channel in force, fulfilling the prediction that "the capital that is being banished from France will, in all probability, locate itself upon the banks of the Thames."[11] Many Frenchmen were escaping a city thrown into turmoil in February 1848 by a revolution of workers, which forced the abdication of King Louis Philippe and established the Second Republic. In the period of unrest that followed, a savage class war broke out, during which over 10,000 workers were killed—a greater loss of life than occurred during any of the insurrections of 1789. Emerging as president-elect was Prince Louis Napoleon Bonaparte, nephew of Napoleon I, by a landslide majority. His election did not signal the end of unrest, however, and in 1851 he staged a successful coup d'état and emerged as the Emperor Napoleon III.

Figure 20. Page from a Maw & Company catalog, circa 1885, showing a suggestion for an ornamental exterior suitable for a railway station hotel. *Ironbridge Gorge Museum Trust*

Figure 21. Majolica tiling was especially appealing to private railway companies competing in the network building boom throughout the last half of the nineteenth century. This example, furnished by Maw & Company, remains at the Shrub Hill Station in Worcester, formerly property of the Great Western Railway. *Ironbridge Gorge Museum Trust*

Figure 22. The Minton Testimonial Museum and School of Design, Stoke-on-Trent, from an engraving by A. M. Williams, 1860. The School of Design at Stoke-on-Trent was one of the earliest and most successful institutions precipitated by the design reform movement. Plans for the building, which were conceived by A.W.N. Pugin shortly before his death and supervised by Leon Arnoux, were begun in the early 1850s; the building was completed with considerable financial assistance from Herbert Minton, in whose honor it was named following his death in 1858. *Minton Museum, Royal Doulton Ltd.*

Figure 23. Tiles made by student John Bradburn as practical work for a design project, Coalbrookdale School of Art, circa 1895. Founded in 1846, the Coalbrookdale School of Art was prominent among schools of design in the Midlands, which promoted the unity of art and industry. These tiles were probably made at the local Jackfield works of Maw & Company. *Ironbridge Gorge Museum Trust*

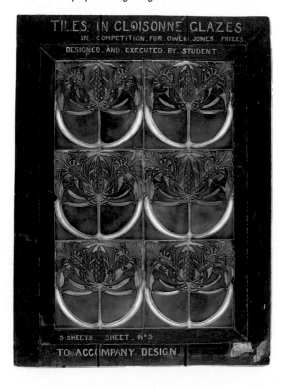

As one would expect with a workers' revolution, the support industries of the wealthy classes suffered drastic consequences, as this contemporary account of the circumstances of Parisian trade illustrates:

> Bankruptcy and beggary prevail in Paris, all who possess anything, and can, even by great sacrifices, convert their property into ready money are flying from a doomed metropolis. Those immense establishments [banks] that employed from three to five hundred clerks and assistants each, are closed.... Trade being at an end, manufacturers are discontinued. Silversmiths send their plate to the mint,... those who are breaking up their establishments are offering their clocks and other articles of furniture at one third of the cost prices.[12]

The consequences of the workers' revolution were profound throughout France and its colonial empire. The immediate removal of wealthy patronage and the decline in French manufacturers, which caused French exports in 1848 to be cut by one-half the totals of the previous year,[13] mirrored the effects of the Revolution of 1789, when French aristocracy—those who escaped with their lives —had fled abroad, many of them to the United States. In 1848, England, with its expanding commercial interests, tradition of affluence and a government and public apparently dedicated to promoting and supporting fine and decorative arts, welcomed French craftsmen and designers.

Among the important majolica designers documented as moving to London as a direct result of disillusionment with the new French system were Albert Ernest Carrier de Belleuse (1824–1887), a modeler of exceptional talent who was "obliged to leave France after taking part in the abortive June revolution of 1849,"[14] and Pierre Emile Jeannest (1813–1857), who had "obtained celebrity" in Paris prior to the revolution and by the summer of 1848 had established himself as an independent designer "on the banks of the

Thames" in London's Percy Street. The most valuable French exile was Leon Arnoux, whose services "Herbert Minton was so fortunate to secure . . . after the troubles of 1848."[15] Arnoux quickly recruited Jeannest and Carrier to join the already highly respected staff of Minton's art department. The confluence of French and English talent that resulted produced a flood of decorative ceramic art that carried Minton into the twentieth century. Almost immediately, this unique union between two countries that had traditionally opposed each other in every ideology, including art, gave birth to a new school of Anglo-French design and created a distinct style recognized by the Staffordshire potters, notably Minton, which nurtured and promoted the style through a variety of decorative ceramics, including majolica ware (Figure 24).

The Anglo-French unification encouraged by Minton and others was a crucial element in the development of Victorian decorative arts, the history of which, like the history of all design, is evolutionary, punctuated by catalytic individuals or groups who work progressively and thus set new standards for others to follow. The influence of such movements can sometimes only be measured in retrospect. This is surely the case with the Staffordshire majolica manufacturers who, collectively, provided such an impetus and steered a course in ceramic design away from convention and toward a whimsical unknown, in a manner that has commonly been considered frivolous but that was, at the core of the movement, at least, carefully controlled and in the best traditions of progressive design in the Potteries.

The sources that inspired designers of English majolica were as varied as the products that emerged from their studios. The following chapter examines the principal design sources and trends in order to render an accurate perception of the chronological progression of taste in the "majolica period," which can be of invaluable assistance in dating and appreciating the ware.

Figure 24. Minton majolica vase in the Anglo-French taste, date code for 1870, height 15". A good example, with typical coloration, of the Anglo-French style developed at Minton by Albert Ernst Carrier de Belleuse and Pierre Emile Jeannest, to whom this vase is attributed. *Collection of Mr. & Mrs. G. Leberfeld*

Figure 25. Design for a saltcellar by Pierre Emile Jeannest, 1848; the elaborate treatment in this model was considered "too pronouncedly French for entire adoption" by contemporary British critics. This sentiment, coupled with the unique combination of French and English talent, led to the emergence of a new academic style by the time of the Great Exhibition in 1851. *Reprinted from* The Art Journal of London, *Annual Edition, 1848*

2

English Majolica
and the Evolution of Style

The Anglo-French Style and Formal Taste

Pierre Emile Jeannest's style was typical of the uniquely French revivalist taste, which celebrated the flamboyance of a rococo past but remained sophisticated and controlled through sincere dedication to classical, academic training in the use of ornament and principles of line (Figure 25). The early designs from his London studio, most of which were intended to be rendered in silver, were praised by English critics for their "appropriate choice of suggestive motifs" but considered "of a character too pronouncedly French for entire adoption."[1] Contemporary popular taste in English decorative arts was derived largely from the same sources that inspired Jeannest and his followers, including the Renaissance and the later style of the Holy Roman Empire, from which many Renaissance motifs were derived (Figure 26), but was typically flawed by a lack of originality, a phenomenon that drew sharp contemporary criticism from such progressive designers as Sir Henry Cole and the architect Augustus Pugin (1812–1852).

Henry Cole welcomed the inventiveness of French designers and attempted to improve the state of English decorative arts through a promotional venture entitled Summerly's Art Manufacturers, dedicated to "connecting the best art with familiar objects in daily use." Cole founded the organization in 1847 under his pseudonym Felix Summerly and commissioned designs for "familiar objects" from prominent manufacturers and members of academic fine arts circles. The finished works were promoted by Summerly's in its *Art Journal*, and when they were sold, part of the proceeds were retained for the organization's benefit. The work of John Bell (Figures 27 and 28), who modeled for Minton and Wedgwood, was frequently

Figure 26. Design for a water jug in silver, by Henry Fitz-Cook, London, 1848. At the time of the arrival of French design talent in England, following the Paris Revolution, popular English taste drew its inspiration from the same historic sources that appealed to the French but was more traditional, authentic, and reserved in execution. *Reprinted from* The Art Journal of London, *Annual Edition, 1848*

Figure 27. Two examples of the "Dolphin" table salt, *above*, modeled by John Bell for Wedgwood, in majolica (*left*) and enameled pearlware (*right*), impressed marks circa 1879 and 1850, respectively, height 4½". The work of English sculptor John Bell is typically in the inspired and controlled revivalist taste of the best French modelers of the day, and it found favor among contemporary critics, notably Henry Cole. Bell's designs were commissioned by a number of Staffordshire potters, including Minton and Copeland. This is one of two models commissioned by Wedgwood, the other being a spill vase.

Figure 28. Printed mark of the modeler John Bell, *left*, beneath a monogram FS, indicating an object made for Felix Summerly's Art Manufacturers. A short-lived promotional concern, Summerly's was initiated by Henry Cole.

Figure 29. Wedgwood majolica jug, *above*, of Anglo-French style, impressed marks and date code for 1869, height 11″. The earlier Wedgwood majolica designed under the Anglo-French influence is typically more reserved in taste than the flamboyant creations of Minton. *Collection of Mr. & Mrs. G. Leberfeld*

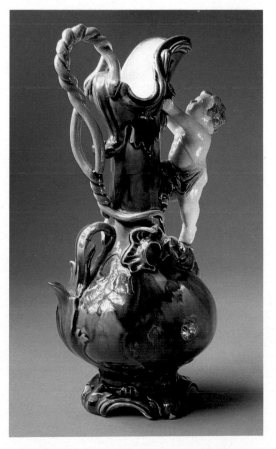

Figure 30. Joseph Holdcroft majolica ewer, *right*, in Rococo Revival taste, circa 1875, height 10¼″. Many of the smaller manufacturers, which did not have the capacity to employ talented foreign designers, produced Rococo Revival ware of significantly less interest than the Anglo-French style of the larger makers. *Collection of Dr. & Mrs. Howard Silby*

represented by Summerly's and his style displays a liberal attitude akin to Jeannest's. Henry Cole's venture lasted only three years and collapsed under criticism of the conflict of interest inferred by Cole's dual roles as commercial promoter and government official. Under the appointment of his friend, Prince Albert, his governmental duties included the first directorship of the South Kensington Museum (now called the Victoria & Albert, where a new addition was recently named in Cole's honor), the core collection of which was formed from the detritus of the Great Exhibition. Summerly's set a precedent, however, that was continued by the Art Union into the 1870s, although most later commissions were for small-scale reproductions of existing sculpture in Parian ware and few original designs were conceived.

Pugin took an equally reactionary stance against what he perceived as the deplorable state of English decorative arts, blaming this, in part, on the design reform movement itself and arguing that British schools of design could not produce "a single artist capable of designing anything original or appropriate." Pugin drew his design ideals from an idealized medieval past and was a figure of enormous influence in the Gothic revival movement of the 1840s, through writings[2] and accomplishments in design that were seeds from which the English Arts and Crafts movement blossomed. Among other singular accomplishments, Pugin designed ceramics in Gothic taste for Minton's in the late 1840s, at least one of which was later produced in majolica (Figure 82). The contemporary influence of Cole's followers and the Gothic Revivalists on industrial arts was limited, however, and greatly overshadowed by the influx of French talent.

The new Anglo-French style was fundamentally an academic one, created by individuals trained in the history of ornament and the principles of "taste" as defined by William Hogarth in the eighteenth century and interpreted by academies of Art and Design ever since.

The best examples of Anglo-French majolica were manufactured by Minton under Leon Arnoux, who commissioned Pierre Emile Jeannest and Albert Carrier as modelers in 1848 and 1849, respectively. Although Jeannest left Minton's employ in 1854 to pursue a career as a designer of silver plate at Elkington's, in Birmingham, prior to his death in 1857, and Carrier left full-time employment at Minton's the following year to return to France, the two were the first of a succession of talented Frenchmen who made the Anglo-French style identifiable with Minton's and exerted their influence upon the Staffordshire Potteries by working for other manufacturers and educating students at local art institutes. Other French artists who painted or modeled majolica ware for Minton's included Victor Simeon, modeler of the

"Prometheus" exhibition vase (Figure 152), who worked from about 1850–1860; Hughes Protat, who replaced Albert Carrier as Minton's chief modeler in 1855, instructed at the Stoke School of Design and was employed by Wedgwood, after 1858, on a free-lance basis; Antonin Boullemier (1840–1900), a figure painter who came from Sèvres in 1872 and remained until his death; Paul Comolera, a modeler specializing in large majolica animal figures at Minton's from 1873 to 1880; and Emile Lessore (1805–1876), better known as a painter for Wedgwood, where he moved in 1862 after four years of employment under Leon Arnoux. In addition to this impressive list, Minton employed a number of uniquely talented French artists for porcelain decoration, most of them trained at the Sèvres factory, notably Louis Marc Emmanuel Solon (1835–1913), the famous *pâte-sur-pâte* artist and ceramic scholar who worked there from 1870 to 1904. Solon married Maria Arnoux, "the boss's daughter," in 1873.

English majolica in the Anglo-French academic style or of "English Rococo" type falls into a general design school that can be considered "formal," a category that also includes all majolica of neoclassical inspiration. Classical art and decoration had been the primary influence for formal English design for a century prior to the manufacture of majolica, but the early Victorians enjoyed a totally different and, arguably, more enlightened perception of classicism than the stark, white marble structures and sculpture and the delicate, pastel-colored fresco paintings that had appealed to Georgian aristocracy. New archaeological evidence, coupled with speculative theory, presented a vivid, polychromatic vision of the ancient world that justified Victorian excess in ornamental splendor. The writings of Hittorff[3] (Figure 36) and others provided the respectability of authenticity for neoclassical designs decorated in majolica glazes, and these found immediate favor with an English and colonial bourgeoisie, especially during the later

Figure 31. Wedgwood majolica mantel clock in Anglo-French taste, modeled after a vase design by Hughes Protat, 1872, 13½". The palette and form of this object, used for the Mermaid production vase, made it especially appealing to the French market that was developed by Wedgwood after their successes at the Paris Exhibition of 1867. The clock movement is of Parisian manufacture.

Figure 32. Monumental Wedgwood majolica footed jardiniere, *left*, impressed marks and date code for 1865, height 18". This impressive piece in the Anglo-French taste popularized by Minton was probably modeled by Albert Carrier, who provided models to Wedgwood's commission during the 1860s; some of these were exhibited at the Paris Exhibition of 1862.

Figure 33. "Trentham" vase, *below*, in majolica glazes by Wedgwood, 1869, height 11". A good example of the Anglo-French academic style in a popular design commissioned by Wedgwood from the London sculptor Roland Morris.

Figure 34. Wedgwood majolica candelabrum, *left*, in the "Boucher" pattern, impressed marks and date code for 1870, height 16". A well-modeled design in the Anglo-French taste. The upper section of this design is removable, and the model was available with three or four branches or, with a lid, as a cassolette.

Figure 35. Wedgwood majolica cassolette, *right*, with Cupid stem, impressed marks and date code for 1873, height 9½". Cassolettes, having a small cover that could be reversed to form a candle nozzle, popular during the third quarter of the eighteenth century, were unique majolica products of the Wedgwood company.

1860s and 1870s, when neoclassicism, usually in the form of Louis XVI revivalism, was universally favored. During this period, even Parian ware, the great Victorian ceramic achievement, was frequently enriched with gilt or even polychrome enamels to render the marblelike white body more appealing to contemporary taste. Among majolica manufacturers, the Wedgwood Company, with its enormous resources of superb neoclassical designs, were uniquely equipped to capitalize upon this trend (Figure 38).

In some respects, this wealth of existing models hindered the progressive potential of Wedgwood's designers. Old forms were simply reintroduced or loosely interpreted and finished in majolica glazes, with little regard for compatibility. That common tendency, of which all manufacturers were guilty, relegates some neoclassical majolica into the whirlpool of Victorian revivalism, which cannot be considered progressive design. This somewhat derogatory distinction cannot be applied to all formal majolica, however. The best examples of Anglo-French taste, for example, while clearly revivalist in ornament, exhibit the spirit of a new and vital movement.

Other examples of formal majolica include objects made in the family of designs intended as tasteful reproductions of Italian Renaissance ceramics, most of which were manufactured in the early majolica period, including large platters of *Urbino* type first produced at Minton before 1851 (Figure 3). The few examples of English majolica in Egyptian taste can also be considered formal. The fashion for decorative motifs derived from ancient Egyptian art and architecture had appeared on a limited scale in eighteenth-century Europe and had considerable impact on the style of the French Empire under Napoleon I, inspired by images of the ancient culture brought from the emperor's successful Egyptian campaigns. Under Napoleon III and the "Second Empire," the style was popularly revived. The demand generated from this fashion and from contemporary discoveries by European and American archaeologists in Egypt accounted for the few majolica designs of Egyptian inspiration, most of which were old models reintroduced by Wedgwood (Figures 42 and 43), although other manufacturers contributed. Of these, George Jones offered a candlestick of sphinx form and a jardiniere with winged sphinx supports (Figure 44).[4]

Figure 36. Greek temple facade, *above*, as envisaged by Jakob-Ignaz Hittorff, reprinted from his profusely illustrated *Restitution du Temple d'Empedocle à Selinant*, 1828. During the second quarter of the nineteenth century, archaeological discoveries in the ancient world prompted new perceptions of the appearance of Greek and Roman architecture and sculpture. The publications of Hittorff and others promoted this polychromatic vision.

Figure 37. Wedgwood majolica jardiniere stand, *right*, in the "Corinthian" pattern, impressed marks and date code for 1877, height 24½". Neoclassical design found little favor among the patrons of English majolica, who preferred the flamboyant, revived styles of the Renaissance and Rococo. A few examples of "true majolica" of neoclassical taste were conceived, however, mostly during the period when the Louis XVI style was fashionably revived, between about 1865 and 1875. Also made as an umbrella stand, this model was included in the Wedgwood display at the Paris Exhibition of 1868.

Figure 38. A pair of Wedgwood majolica "Wine and Water" ewers, *left*, 1867, height 17". This highly impressive pair of decorative ewers, after the eighteenth-century model popularly attributed to John Flaxman, was the most expensive production model in Wedgwood's majolica catalog of 1876. The traditional perception of classical ornament and coloration as depicted in Wedgwood's neoclassical ware of the late eighteenth century was dramatically altered by contemporary thought in the mid-nineteenth century, which gave credibility to the combination of classical form and polychrome. Wedgwood exploited this by reviving a number of its eighteenth-century models (originally made in refined stonewares) with majolica glazes.

Figure 39. Minton majolica jardiniere, *below*, of trough form, circa 1865, length 12½". A fine and unusual example, in formal Louis XVI taste, intended for use as a table ornament. *Collection of Dr. & Mrs. Howard Silby*

Figure 40. Wedgwood majolica jardiniere stand, *left*, in neoclassical (Louis XVI revival) taste, impressed marks and date code for 1891, height 9½". The neoclassical taste continued in popularity throughout the 1890s and was especially popular in Edwardian Britain. *Collection of Mr. & Mrs. G. Leberfeld*

Figure 41. Wedgwood majolica platter, *above*, depicting Thetis, a sea nymph, and the mother of Achilles, with serpent emerging from the sea, impressed marks and date code for 1871, diameter 15". The Wedgwood Company exploited its vast resources of neoclassical ornament in the production of formal majolica.

Figure 42. Pair of Wedgwood majolica candlesticks, *above left*, in the "Philae" pattern, impressed marks and date code for 1868, height 6¾". Wedgwood had the largest range of majolica ware in Egyptian taste. Much of it, including this design, was made from molds issued during the larger Egyptian revival of the early nineteenth century.

Figure 43. Candlestick, *above*, in Egyptian taste by Wedgwood, impressed marks and date code for 1867, height 10¼". The mottled combination of glazes successfully used on this example had been manufactured by Wedgwood since the mid-eighteenth century but is considered majolica ware at this period.

Figure 44. Design for a "Sphinx" jardiniere, *left*, in majolica by George Jones, circa 1875. One of only two George Jones models in Egyptian taste recorded. *Trustees of the Wedgwood Museum, Barlaston, Staffordshire, England*

The most useful, as well as the most ornamental devices, which have sprung from the exercise of human ingenuity, have all been founded upon the varied and beautiful creations which nature has presented to us.[5]

Robert Hunt, 1848

Majolica in Romantic and Revivalist Taste

Archaeology was not the only science to come under the scrutiny of Victorian scholars. While most of the world's topography had been mapped and explored by the beginning of the nineteenth century, it was the Victorians who recorded its flora, fauna, and oceanic life. These new discoveries precipitated the establishment of museums of natural history and countless volumes of illustrated treatises on the natural sciences as diverse as conchology, the study of mollusks and shells, and entomology, the study of insects. Many majolica designs reflect those current fascinations (Figures 45 and 46), the more conventional of which had attracted ceramic artists for over a century, and all of the larger manufacturers contributed to this category. Some individuals combined a scholarly pursuit of natural sciences with their careers as potters. George Maw was an accomplished botanist and fellow of the Linnaean Society, for which he produced a magnificently illustrated treatise on the *genus crocus*, examples of which can be traced in his tile designs. Louis Jahn (1840–1911), who worked as art director for William Brownfield and Sons and, later, for Minton's, was an authority on local beetles, which he often spent afternoons hunting.[6]

The most celebrated Victorian naturalist was, of course, Charles Darwin (1809–1882); it is not

Figure 45. Pair of Wedgwood majolica table salts, *above*, in the "Cockle" pattern, impressed marks and date code for 1871, height 3½". A good example of Victorian seaside ware, this naturalistic model was also offered in majolica catalogs as a "trinket" holder.

Figure 46. "Fly" matchbox, *above*, in Wedgwood majolica, impressed marks and date code for 1876, length 5". Wedgwood offered a range of fourteen matchboxes in 1876. In this example, the wings lift off to reveal a striker beneath and a hollow body to hold matches. Naturalistically modeled fly ornaments were made contemporaneously in cast iron and brass and reflect the popularity of entomology in the 1870s.

Figure 47. Wedgwood majolica umbrella stand, *left*, of naturalistic form, impressed marks and date code for 1882, height 21".

Figure 48. Detail of one of the two green woodpeckers, *below*, modeled in naturalistic relief in Figure 47.

Figure 49. The taste for naturalism in a design drawing showing the full complement of items in a George Jones majolica dressing set, *opposite*, circa 1875. Each of these items was available separately. The applied butterflies on several items were optional extras. The Pomade box is intended to hold face or hair cream. *Trustees of the Wedgwood Museum, Barlaston, Staffordshire, England*

Figure 50. Wedgwood dessert plate, *left*, with botanical and ornithological printed decoration and majolica-glazed rim, impressed marks and date code for 1888, diameter 9″. Wedgwood continued to produce ware with majolica glazes longer than any of its rivals. This attractive design, effectively combining two decorating techniques, displays the off-white body of the Queens ware type from which most Wedgwood majolica was made.

Figure 51. Design for a "Giraffe" center (footed center bowl), *right*, in majolica by George Jones, circa 1879. The boldest and rarest of George Jones centers. This model, which illustrates the contemporary passion for natural history, represented Africa in a series of four designs with naturalistic stems allegorical of continents. *Trustees of the Wedgwood Museum, Barlaston, Staffordshire, England*

so well known that he was related to the Wedg-wood family by marriage. Darwin's original position as official naturalist aboard the exploration ship H.M.S. *Beagle* in the 1830s led to his epoch-making publication *On the Origin of Species* in 1859. The theoretical work met with enormous opposition from a religious and moralist front, largely due to the implications of man being related to apes, and the controversy that ensued filled the popular press of several countries. It is likely that several of the more bizarre English majolica designs that include members of the ape family as motifs were intended as derisive commentary upon Darwin's theories. It was common practice among the Staffordshire potters to fashion topical images for commercial reasons and, in most cases, including the design for a garden seat illustrated as Figure 53, the primates depicted are of African or South American type and predate the main period of Japanese influence in English ceramics when monkey motifs became more commonplace. The unique products of Bernard Palissy (1510–1590), the great French potter and naturalist, inspired a number of English majolica designs, although most of his imitators worked in France (see chapter 6). Outstanding among this group is the Palissy vase by George Jones (Figures 59 and 60), which is the only model of this class from that manufacturer. The glazes and technical abilities of Palissy were of enormous influence in the work of Leon Arnoux, and some Palissy designs were reproduced at Minton's in the early majolica period.

Formal styles dominated the majolica output of Minton's and Wedgwood, although all manufacturers produced majolica in the Romantic taste, exploring the sensations of a pre-industrial era—or the wonders of nature—which Victorian scholars delighted in discovering and revealing. A unique development of this movement was the continuation of a Romantic style of figure modeling, which had been developed by the Wood family of pot-

Figure 52. Minton majolica jug, date code for 1869, height 12¼". A good example of an innovative form derived from the contemporary trend for using organic (leaf) forms in modeling. *Collection of Mr. & Mrs. G. Leberfeld*

ters and their followers in Staffordshire at the end of the eighteenth century (Figures 62, 63, and 64). The naive, distinctly English style, which was originally manifested in creamware or pearlware with decoration in colored glazes, translated well into majolica ware. Minton's and others designed figural objects in this style (Figures 66 and 67), while some manufacturers reduced the expense of putting new designs into production by reintroducing old models with majolica glazes. This was an especially popular practice among smaller manufacturers.

Revivalism is the common denominator in Victorian design and was considered respectable in any tasteful manifestation, including interpretations or facsimiles of historical styles and objects. The design and production of ceramics was not exempt; indeed, the ware's general popularity and many of the specific forms introduced during the early majolica period can be directly attributed

to the advocates of revivalist taste and a new social consumer class precipitated by the rapid urbanization and growth of industry in the mid-nineteenth century. The new wealthy built extensive suburban and country homes, many boasting conservatories that were fashionably furnished with majolica stools, jardinieres, and wall pockets (Figures 69, 70, 71, and 73). Majolica usage was not limited to hothouses, however:

> The majolica ware is very fashionable now, and dessert, oyster, and salads sets of it are exceedingly pretty.[7]

The contemporary passion for formal entertaining made a profusion of majolica tableware popular, including centerpieces (Figures 74 and 75) and items designed for the cooking and serving of seafood, the new railway networks having made fresh seafood available to even the most provincial host (Figures 57, 61, and 77). In the 1860s, the British discovered the charms of their own extensive coastline and, as the Victorian seaside resorts flourished, the makers of majolica met the incessant demand for trinkets and souvenirs from enthusiastic tourists (Figures 79, 80, and 81).

Gothic and Medieval styles appealed principally to the puritanical spirit and the liberal ideals shared by followers of Britain's emerging Arts and Crafts movement, while romantic naturalism enjoyed a more general favor. Most majolica in the Gothic or Medieval taste was designed by Minton's, which had the largest repertoire of all majolica manufacturers. The styles were found especially suitable for architectural majolica and all forms of building ornament (Figure 83), but a significant amount of ware in the category was also made. Jugs and drinking mugs for ale, modeled in a combination of the early nineteenth-century Staffordshire Romantic style and the contemporary "Troubadour"[8] or Medieval Revival style (Figures 85, 86, and 87) proved commercially successful at home and in continental Europe. Precise renderings of Gothic, Medieval, Elizabethan, and even Celtic ornament, as supplied by Owen Jones,[9] sometimes appear on majolica ware, but the influence is more typically present in the discreet use of motifs, sometimes in incongruous combination with other elements. Owen Jones's compendium of design, *The Grammar of Ornament*, published in 1856, provided manufacturers with a comprehensive record of ornamental art from the ancient world, the Near and Far East, "savage tribes," the Middle Ages, and the Renaissance and was of enormous influence in majolica design, especially for tiles (Figures 90–93).

Figure 53. Pair of Minton majolica garden seats, *right*, each in the form of a seated monkey supporting a cushion, impressed marks and date code for 1873, height 18¼". A variety of Minton designs featuring monkeys in extraordinary postures were made in majolica ware from the late 1850s, coinciding with the publication of Darwin's *On the Origin of Species*. This model, which leaves no doubt as to the relative position of ape and man, may have been designed in support of the contemporary criticism of Darwin's theory. *Sotheby's, New York*

Figure 54. Original design drawing for the monkey garden seat, *above*, circa 1859 (majolica design number 440) from Minton majolica rag books. Such rag books, including crudely drawn images with design numbering details, were intended as pattern books for everyday use. A comprehensive series of them survives in the Minton Archives and provides a remarkable record of the company's majolica output. *Minton Museum, Royal Doulton Ltd.*

Figure 55. Minton majolica teapot, *above*, in the form of a monkey clutching a coconut, impressed marks and date code for 1865, height 6½". *Collection of Mr. & Mrs. G. Leberfeld*

Figure 56. Minton majolica lobster tureen, *left*, impressed marks and date code for 1870, length 14″. Bold, naturalistic representation of creatures in glazed earthenware as practiced by Bernard Palissy was especially suitable for the design of seafood serving pieces, and ware of this type can be ascribed to Palissy influence. *Collection of Mr. & Mrs. G. Leberfeld*

Figure 57. Wedgwood majolica lobster plate, *above*, impressed marks and date code for 1880, diameter 8½″. *Collection of Mr. & Mrs. G. Leberfeld*

Figure 58. Minton majolica seafood platter, *left*, impressed marks and date code for 1873, length 23″. In this successful design, the concept of modeling crustaceans in full, naturalistic relief is an interpretation of the techniques and style of Bernard Palissy. *Minton Museum, Royal Doulton Ltd.*

Figure 59. George Jones majolica Palissy vase, circa 1868, height 16″. This model is the only example of George Jones majolica executed in the manner of Bernard Palissy. *Britannia, Gray's Antique Market, London*

Figure 60. George Jones drawing for the Palissy vase (design number 1459), illustrated in Figure 59. *Trustees of the Wedgwood Museum, Barlaston, Staffordshire, England*

Figure 61. Wedgwood majolica oyster plate in Palissy style and a mussel plate, *above*, impressed marks and date codes for 1879 and 1878, diameters 9″ and 7¼″, respectively. The variety of seafood that Victorians discovered and enjoyed at resorts soon became acceptable for formal dining, and this precipitated a new market for tableware that was widely exploited by majolica manufacturers.

Figure 62. A pair of pearlware figures of recumbent deer, *right*, in the manner of the Wood family of potters, Staffordshire, circa 1800, height of figure 6½″.

Figure 63. A Staffordshire majolica-glazed figure of a recumbent stag, circa 1875, height 10½", unmarked. This large ornament, presumably one of a pair (to include a doe), is clearly inspired by the glazed earthenware figures of Ralph Wood and his contemporaries, although the large scale alone indicates Victorian manufacture. *Collection of J. Garvin Mecking, Inc.*

Figure 64. Staffordshire majolica-glazed relief plaque, *below*, in Romantic style, circa 1870, 13″ × 10″. Plaques of this type were popular in the early nineteenth century as wall decorations in simple cottages, and a few were made later in the century from old molds with majolica glazes. *Collection of Mr. & Mrs. G. Leberfeld*

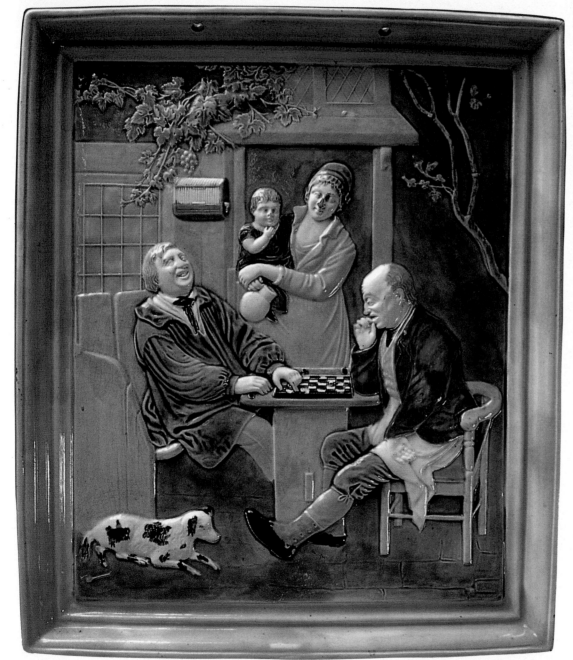

Figure 65. Design for an allegorical figure of Spring, *above*, by Mary Thornycroft, 1848, in Parian. The modeling of this figure, a portrait of Princess Alice, Queen Victoria's eldest daughter, is typical of the Staffordshire Romantic style of the late eighteenth century, which was successfully revived by majolica designers. *Reprinted from* The Art Journal of London, *Annual Edition 1848, p. 148*

Figure 67. A pair of Joseph Holdcroft majolica sweetmeat dishes, *below*, modeled as kneeling women in full skirts, circa 1865, height 6". The Staffordshire Romantic style, which enjoyed wide appeal in the home market, was especially favored by smaller manufacturers. *Collection of Dr. & Mrs. Howard Silby*

Figure 66. Minton majolica pitcher, *above*, modeled as a peasant woman, 1866, height 11¼". A good example of majolica conceived in the Staffordshire Romantic taste. The exposed body color used for flesh tone and the choice of marbleizing to ornament the base are further evidence of the influence of earlier potters. This model was also produced as a jug, with a hinged cover. *Collection of Mr. & Mrs. G. Leberfeld*

Figure 68. Many of the stately suburban homes built for the newly wealthy Victorian class in the U.S. and Britain included conservatories, *opposite*, providing a demand for jardinieres, wall pockets, and hanging pots in majolica. Drawing rooms and ample dining rooms were suitably highlighted with majolica figures, candlesticks, and tableware of all description. *Mark Twain Memorial, Hartford, Connecticut*

Figure 69. George Jones majolica jardiniere, *below*, of a type commonly used in Victorian conservatories or parlors, height 12". *Collection of Mr. & Mrs. G. Leberfeld*

Figure 70. A monumental Minton majolica plant stand, *above*, displayed at the Philadelphia Centennial Exhibition, 1876. Minton excelled in the production of majolica fountains and plant stands that were used as hothouse centerpieces by the newly wealthy.

Figure 71. Wedgwood majolica "Rubens" garden seat for use in a conservatory, impressed marks and date code for 1874, height 17½". Majolica of this type was designed to meet the demands of the new affluent class that was precipitated by rapid industrialization on both sides of the Atlantic and that sought inspiration in the future and emulation in the past. Newly wealthy Victorians filled the conservatories, parlors, and dining rooms of their expansive suburban homes with revivalism for prestige.

Figure 72. Wedgwood majolica strawberry dish with sugar and creamer, *left*, impressed marks and date code for 1871, length 10″. Strawberry dishes by Wedgwood are rare; this is the only recorded model. Their popularity was largely due to the contemporary fashion for hothouses.

Figure 73. Wedgwood majolica "greenhouse bracket", *below*, in the "Cupid" design, 1871, height 9″. A uniquely Victorian object, intended for holding potted plants in a conservatory. The clever modeling is attributed to William Beattie.

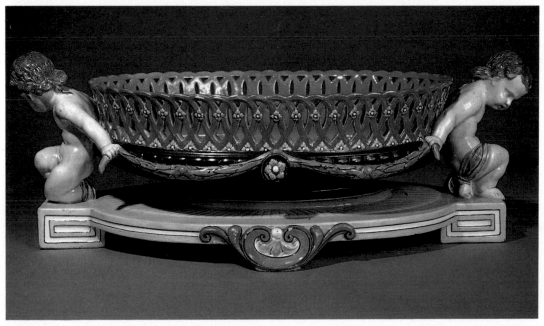

Figure 74. Wedgwood majolica centerpiece, *left*, in the "Eugénie" pattern, impressed marks and date code for 1869, length 19″. A good example of Wedgwood majolica in the Anglo-French taste made for the lavish demands of Victorian hosts. Attributed to Hughes Protat, this design was made with the upper rim pierced or solid.

Figure 75. Wedgwood majolica small cake stand, *left*, in the "Dolphin" pattern, impressed marks and date code for 1878, height 6¾". This popular design was made in several sizes for majolica and had been produced earlier in the century in pearlware. The serving of afternoon tea, for which cake stands were essential, was widely practiced by Victorian hosts.

Figure 76. Wedgwood majolica tea set, *below*, in the "Punch and Judy" pattern, impressed marks and date code for 1879, length of pot 7¾". An extraordinary design featuring the famous sideshow characters who were such great favorites at Victorian seaside resorts.

Figure 77. George Jones majolica-covered mackerel server, *opposite*, circa 1870, length 19". Using the same base, another version of this design featured a salmon motif. George Jones fish servers were made in two sizes, this being the smaller; the larger was 23" in length. *Collection of Dr. & Mrs. Howard Silby*

Figure 78. Wedgwood majolica game pie dish, *opposite below*, suitable for the finest Victorian table, impressed marks and date code for 1870, length 11". Wedgwood had manufactured game pie dishes in caneware that simulated pastry crust in the early nineteenth century, but a half-century later, these were most popular in majolica glazes. Dishes of this type were used to prepare and serve casseroles and "jugged" dishes, as well as pigeon or other game pies. *Collection of Lloyd J. Bleier*

Figure 79. Wedgwood majolica cruet stand, *left*, in the "Clarendon" pattern, impressed marks, circa 1875, diameter of tray 6½". Trinket souvenirs were an essential pursuit in the Victorian passion for visiting seaside resorts, and Wedgwood designed a range of majolica ware for that market. Examples include jars and boxes for fish paste, cigar trays, and other small ornamental ware including this "Clarendon" set named for a famous Victorian resort.

Figure 80. English majolica teapot, *below*, in the form of a three-legged sailor holding an ensign, printed retailer's mark of "W. BROUGHTON, DOUGLAS" (Isle of Man), attributed to Brown-Westhead, Moore & Co., circa 1875, height 8". A good example of English majolica designed as a tourist souvenir, this was probably sold exclusively in Douglas, capital of the Isle of Man, whose coat of arms depicts a three-legged image. *Collection of Mr. & Mrs. G. Leberfeld*

Figure 81. Wedgwood majolica (Argenta ware) butter dish, *left*, in the form of a barrel washed up on the seashore, impressed marks and date code for 1879, length 7½". In this cleverly designed model the hollow base can be filled with crushed ice.

Figure 82. Minton majolica supper tray, the design attributed to A.W.N. Pugin, circa 1849, impressed marks and date code for 1880, diameter 18½". Supper trays with revolving tops, known in the United States as "Lazy Susans," were popular table accessories in mid-Victorian England. This arrangement of Gothic motifs, decorated with majolica glazes and embossed in a simulated tube lining technique, is attributed to the architect and industrial designer A.W.N. Pugin. *J. Garvin Mecking, Inc.*

Figure 83. The taste for historicism in four 6″ × 6″ majolica tiles, *above*, by Minton Hollins & Company, portraying figures from Anglo-Saxon history. *Ironbridge Gorge Museum Trust*

Figure 84. Minton majolica tile in medieval taste, *above*, circa 1878, 6″ × 6″.

Figure 85. Minton majolica "Tower" jug, *right*, with hinged pewter cover, marks and data code for 1872, height 13″. A popular Minton model, designed in the fashionable Medieval Revival taste, intended for the serving of beer. *Collection of Dr. & Mrs. Howard Silby*

Majolica

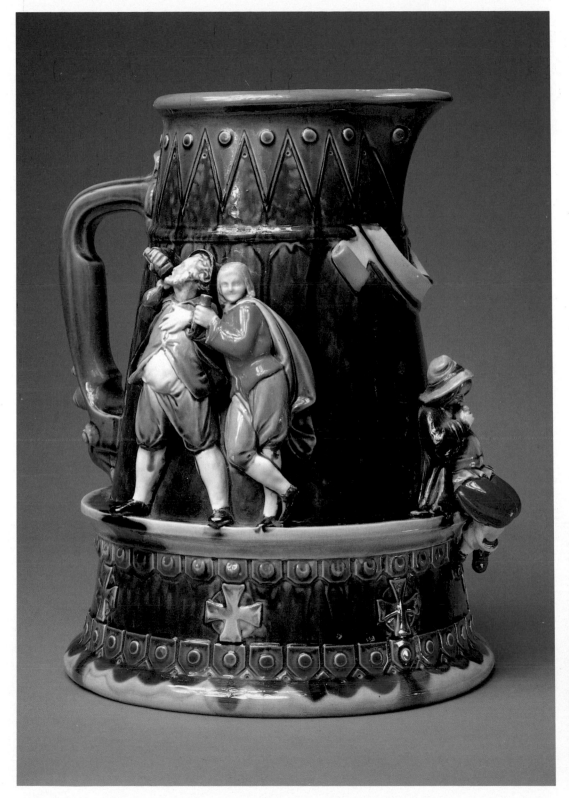

Figure 86. Minton majolica beer jug, *left*, impressed marks and date code for 1861, height 13″. A good example of English majolica in the Medieval Revival taste, favored in the export market of Northern Europe. *Collection of Mr. & Mrs. G. Leberfeld*

Figure 87. Two versions of the popular "Caterer" jug, *below*, in Wedgwood majolica with hinged silver and pewter covers, designed by Frederick Bret Russel, circa 1869; height of the taller jug is 11¼″. Frederick Bret Russel worked in the popular, progressive Aesthetic style of the emerging Arts and Crafts Movement and drew the principal influence of his work from medieval ornament. *Collection of Mr. & Mrs. G. Leberfeld*

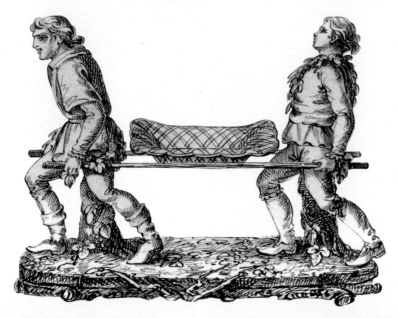

Figure 88. Design for a Minton majolica centerpiece, *left*, in the "Vintagers" pattern, modeled as two grape harvesters, from the Minton majolica rag books, circa 1861. A good example of Minton majolica ware in the Romantic medieval taste. *Minton Museum, Royal Doulton Ltd.*

Figure 89. English majolica sweetmeat dish, *left*, unmarked, circa 1870, height 7". The stag's head motif was frequently employed in the spirit of romanticism that evoked the medieval past. *Collection of Joan Esch; photograph by Gary Samson*

Figure 90. Set of four majolica tiles by Maw & Company, *below*, circa 1880, each 6" × 6". These tiles are typical of the high-quality geometric patterns, derived from Mooresque ornament, as illustrated by Owen Jones. *Ironbridge Gorge Museum Trust*

Figure 91. Minton Hollins & Company majolica wall tile, *above*, of Persian design derived from Owen Jones's *Grammar of Ornament*, circa 1880, 6″ × 6″. *Ironbridge Gorge Museum Trust*

Figure 92. An arrangement of Craven Dunhill embossed majolica tiles, *above*, in Persian taste, circa 1880. *Ironbridge Gorge Museum Trust*

Figure 93. Design for a George Jones majolica jardiniere, *right*, in neoclassical taste, circa 1880. This model incorporates Greek motifs (as illustrated by Owen Jones) in a treatment similar to the style of Dr. Christopher Dresser and evidences George Jones's broad repertoire of designs. *Trustees of the Wedgwood Museum, Barlaston, Staffordshire, England*

Oriental-Style Majolica and *Japonisme*

Many sources of majolica designs can be traced to the manufacturer's library of illustrated art books, which could be freely copied, on such subjects as botany, natural history, and ornithology as well as classical and Renaissance art and architecture and Chinese and Japanese art, ceramics and woodblock prints. Several of the volumes were brought to the Minton library by Leon Arnoux,[10] including those on the subject of Chinese decorative arts, which was his personal interest. The design influence from Chinese ceramic art is occasionally evident in Minton majolica ware, although it is more commonly found in contemporary Minton porcelain. There is no doubt, how-ever, that several familiar Minton designs, notably those for garden stools, are derived directly from these source books. Perhaps the most ambitious majolica project in Chinese taste was the design of a chair of Mandarin type (which was probably never executed),[11] inspired by a Chinese lacquered wood chair illustrated in one of Arnoux's volumes[12] (Figure 96).

It is important not to confuse the use of Chinese motifs or those derived from the natural sciences and the Victorian passion for discovery with other forms of naturalistic ornament used under the influence of *Japonisme*, the Western interpretation of Japanese art and design. The first European exhibition of Japanese art was held in London in 1854, followed by a larger and more significant showing in 1867, and the ensuing wave of Western taste for Japanese style indicated the opening of Japan to be the most significant single influence upon Western decorative arts in the nineteenth century. The first exhibitions of Japanese art in England were largely limited to small and highly sophisticated objects, most of them antiques, in the traditional crafts of ivory carving, metalwork, woodblock printing, and potting. From these objects majolica designers derived a knowledge of Japanese flora and fauna, as well as vase forms, all of which held relatively little interest within the popular marketplaces. By the 1870s, however, Japan had developed its own export industry and was exhibiting its wares at international exhibitions alongside those of Western manufacturers. The new Japanese industry produced ceramics, metalwork, furniture, graphic designs, and ivories of a style and scale that was eagerly consumed throughout western Europe and the United States, and it is this taste that is commonly found in majolica (Figures 98–104). Insects, ex-

otic fish, mice, frogs, lizards, and flying cranes were all popular emblems of *Japonisme*, as were familiar Japanese flora, notably the chrysanthemum and *prunus* blossoms.

Despite the overwhelming influence of the Japanese export style, the true principles of traditional Japanese design were recognized by serious Victorian scholars on the decorative arts, who found the achievement of beauty through simplicity of form, materials, and manufacture to represent a fresh and revolutionary attitude. These principles and their implications to Western design, as published by Charles Locke Eastlake (1836–1906),[13] were the fundamental concerns of the school of design we now call the Aesthetic Movement, which had little contemporary impact upon popular decorative arts, especially in majolica production, but is considered, in retrospect, to have had extreme and far-reaching social and artistic influence, especially in America, where it "affected all levels of society," according to a recent retrospective study.[14]

The few majolica products to exhibit Aesthetic taste are typically patterned with formalized flora of a type introduced by Walter Crane (1845–1915) and others, and most are of Wedgwood manufacture (Figures 105–111). The most celebrated English designer in the Aesthetic style was Dr. Christopher Dresser (1834–1904), who was prolific in his work for several potteries, including Wedgwood and Minton's, where he is recorded as having produced designs for majolica,[15] although no majolica by Dresser is known, and it is unlikely that any was ever produced.

Figure 94. Joseph Holdcroft majolica teapot, *opposite left*, in Chinese taste, circa 1875. Height 7". *Collection of Mr. & Mrs. G. Leberfeld*

Figure 95. Minton majolica teapot, *opposite right*, in Chinese taste, date code for 1876, length 7". *Collection of Mr. & Mrs. G. Leberfeld*

Figure 96. Design for a majolica chair, *above*, in Chinese taste (Minton design number 242), circa 1860. An ambitious project which was probably never realized, although majolica furniture of Chinese inspiration in the form of garden stools was extensively produced by Minton and others. *Minton Museum, Royal Doulton Ltd.*

Figure 97. Copeland majolica milk jug, *left*, in the form of a seated Mandarin, circa 1875, height 4½". A good example of the contemporary taste for chinoiserie, this attractive object is slip-cast in Copeland's popular "Ivory" body, the natural color of which is exposed for the flesh of this model. *Collection of J. Garvin Mecking, Inc.*

Figure 98. Japanese cloisonné enamel plate or tray, *left*, patterned with flying cranes, exhibited at the Philadelphia Exhibition of 1876.

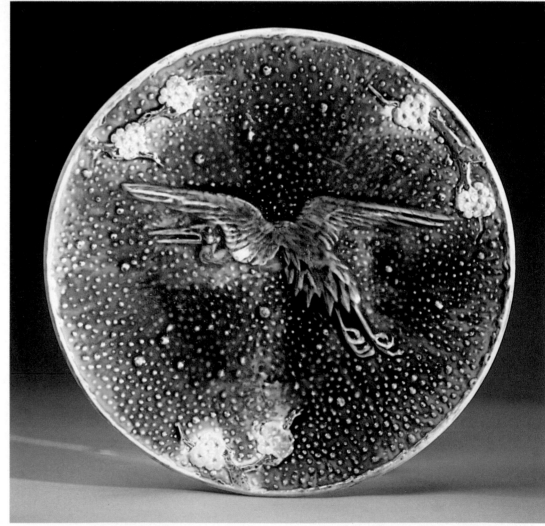

Figure 99. Joseph Holdcroft majolica plate, *right*, patterned with flying cranes, impressed marks, circa 1877, diameter 8″. The Japanese export style was enormously successful at the Philadelphia Centennial Exhibition and at contemporary exhibitions in Europe, and a variety of English majolica in Japanese taste was produced for domestic and foreign markets. *Collection of Dr. & Mrs. Howard Silby*

Figure 100. Wedgwood majolica oval tray in Japanese taste, impressed marks and date code for 1879, length 14".

Figure 101. Japanese bronze jardiniere in the Export style, *above left*, circa 1875.

Figure 102. Wedgwood majolica luncheon plate, *above*, in the "Fan" pattern, impressed marks and date code for 1879, diameter 9¼". *Collection of Denny and Elaine Lotwin*

Figure 103. A majolica oval platter, *left*, in Japanese taste, by Simon Fielding & Co., circa 1881, impressed registry mark, length 13". A good example of the high quality in design and manufacture achieved by notable but generally anonymous Staffordshire manufacturers of majolica. *Collection of Dr. & Mrs. Howard Silby*

Figure 104. "Bamboo" design card tray, *above*, in Wedgwood majolica, impressed marks and date code for 1872, diameter 10¼". Intended to hold calling cards of acquaintances, card trays were requisite in the entrance halls of the Victorian social class. This model was available in three sizes (this being the mid-size), which, presumably, indicated a measure of the owner's popularity.

Figure 105. A section of iron railing, *above*, designed in the Aesthetic taste, English, circa 1876. The concept of naturalistic motifs depicted in a stylized manner and formalized arrangement can be found in a variety of decorative arts from the mid-1870s, including the work of Walter Crane (1845–1915). A small amount of majolica ware was conceived in this style, mostly by Wedgwood, but few examples were made after about 1885.

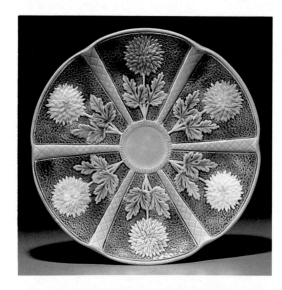

Figure 106. Wedgwood majolica dessert plate, *above*, in the Aesthetic taste, impressed marks and date code for 1882, diameter 9″.

Figure 107. Copeland majolica jug, *above*, of four-gill (one pint) capacity patterned with formalized water lilies in Aesthetic taste, impressed marks and registry mark for 1872, height 8″. *Collection of Mr. & Mrs. G. Leberfeld*

Figure 108. Majolica wall tile, *left*, in Aesthetic taste by Pilkington's Tile and Pottery Company, circa 1885, 6″ × 6″. Most manufacturers of "Art Tiles" practiced the popular technique of "tube-lining," whereby a design was piped by hand onto a surface in liquid clay (slip); the resulting "pools" were filled with majolica-type glazes. This tile simulates the technique, forming an embossed "tube-lined" outline by conventional pressing. *Ironbridge Gorge Museum Trust*

Figure 109. Two embossed majolica tiles, *right*, in Aesthetic taste by Minton Hollins & Company, of simple repeating design, circa 1880, each 6″ × 6″. *Ironbridge Gorge Museum Trust*

Figure 110. Wedgwood majolica dessert plate, *opposite*, in the "Orange" pattern, impressed marks and date code for 1880, diameter 8¾". The Aesthetic style derived much of its appeal from the implementation of new perceptions learned from Japanese art regarding the placement and perspective of motifs in design. *Collection of Mr. & Mrs. G. Leberfeld*

Figure 111. Minton majolica teapot, *right*, impressed mark and date code for 1872, length 7½". This extraordinary design combines the progressive taste of *Japonisme* in the Aesthetic style and Victorian whimsy at its most charming. It is clearly the work of a commissioned designer working from outside the Minton factory. *Collection of Joan Esch; photograph by Gary Samson*

3

Color is to the eye
as music to the ear.

Louis Comfort Tiffany

The Making of Majolica

Figure 112. Leon Arnoux, "The man who made Minton's," circa 1890. *Minton Museum, Royal Doulton Ltd.*

Glazes, Kilns, and the Genius of Leon Arnoux

In ceramics, glazing is, simply put, the application of superficial layers of glasslike material over a vitrified or unvitrified body for decorative effect or to achieve an impervious barrier. Decorative ceramics have traditionally been covered with a transparent or translucent glaze to exploit surface decoration, and even the colored glazes used in Staffordshire up until the mid-nineteenth century were mostly translucent. Majolica glazes are distinct in that they are usually opaque, and thus an object applied with them achieves its ornament from the color combination of glazes and not from anything beneath or over them. The development of attractive majolica glazes was thus crucial to the success of the ware and represents one of the few identifiable innovations in the Staffordshire Potteries since the eighteenth century.

For their majolica colors, Minton's relied entirely on a spectrum of glazes devised by Leon Arnoux during his first years of employment there. All colors in ceramic artistry are achieved by the reaction of metals or minerals during firing and cooling, and glazes are simply glass compounds with reactive elements added. Formulas, or "recipes," for glazes of all types were common knowledge in Victorian Staffordshire, but the secret of Arnoux's success was the development of a series of colored glazes that reacted into vibrant colors within the same temperature range, roughly 900–1100°C, and were compatible with each other and the underlying body. In order to produce Minton's magnificent majolica, Arnoux could not settle for the traditional palette of *gros feu* colors of the decorative ceramics industry—cobalt blue, green, "manganese" purple, yellow, and "iron" red. Through meticulous experiments, re-

Figure 113. Minton majolica jardiniere, *left*, in the familiar palette of colored glazes developed by Leon Arnoux, molded with relief profile plaques representing Africa and America (*verso*), impressed marks and date code for 1869, height 13½″. One of a pair of jardinieres representing the continents (the other example featuring Europe and Asia) that may have been made for an international exhibition. The allegorical medallions were also produced individually (see Figure 114) by Minton for use in architectural ornament. *Britannia, Gray's Antique Market, London*

Figure 114. Detail of the Africa medallion, *below*, in Figure 113. *Britannia, Gray's Antique Market, London*

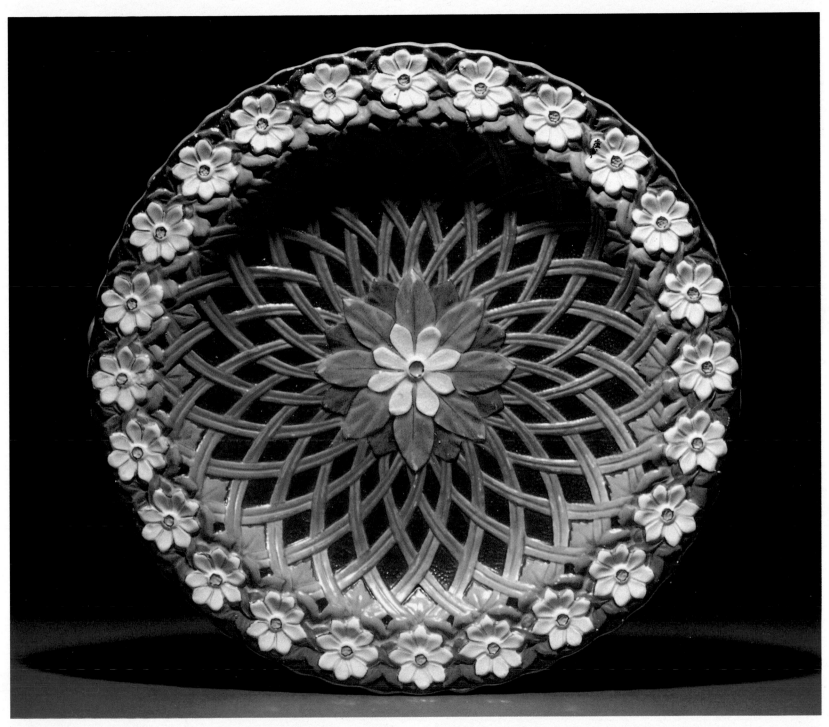

Figure 115. A George Jones majolica jardiniere, *opposite*, circa 1875. A fine example of "true majolica" in a uniquely Victorian object. Most smaller majolica manufacturers in Staffordshire copied the palette of glazes developed by Arnoux. George Jones was especially successful in this area of production. *Collection of Mr. & Mrs. G. Leberfeld*

Figure 116. Minton majolica large platter, *above*, designed circa 1860, diameter 12½". Leon Arnoux's extensive range of majolica glazes included several distinct shades of green, which could be used in combination. The darker green in the central florette is Arnoux's "Magellan." *Collection of J. Garvin Mecking, Inc.*

corded in the glaze trial notebooks he kept by hand between 1849 and 1850,[1] Arnoux perfected the colored glazes to which the term "majolica" was immediately given, and which were subsequently copied throughout the industry with varying degrees of success. Some of Arnoux's glazes, with their active ingredients, include *vert bleu*, a blue-green made by combining carbonate of cobalt and chromium oxide; *brun chocolat*, the rich, chocolate brown frequently used as a ground or in mottled wares, made from manganese and borax; *bleu clair*, the distinctive pale blue of Minton; turquoise, yellow, white, purple, and a rich sea green which Arnoux termed Magellan[2] (Figures 113, 114, and 115).

Arnoux's experimental work on glazes and the formulation of compatible bodies, or "pastes," required exhaustive testing, all of which was carried out in conditions devised by Arnoux. The ultimate results of his efforts were fired in Minton's majolica kilns, built after Arnoux's own design perfected during this experimental period, using kiln furniture and specialized refractory ware also conceived by Arnoux.[3] In some cases, glazes were subjected to over twenty test firings, as was the case for the turquoise color, which proved extremely troublesome to perfect,[4] varying one or more ingredients by minute amounts in different glaze recipes with each firing. Victory over the trial and error involved in this process is testament to the diligence of Leon Arnoux. His abilities as a glaze chemist and master ceramicist were confirmed by the results, which established Arnoux as a singular achiever in the history of English ceramics, irrespective of his contributions to artistic design and kiln technology. Other factories did not have access to the ability of "the man who made Minton's," as Arnoux came to be known in the Potteries toward the end of his career. Wedgwood drew from its legacy of superior glaze recipes, dating back to the early achievements of Josiah Wedgwood I and his contemporaries, and made

Figure 117. Creamware coffee pot of cauliflower design, Staffordshire, circa 1760, height 13″. The lustrous green glaze developed by Josiah Wedgwood I and his contemporaries proved highly suitable for majolica-glazed wares a century later.

 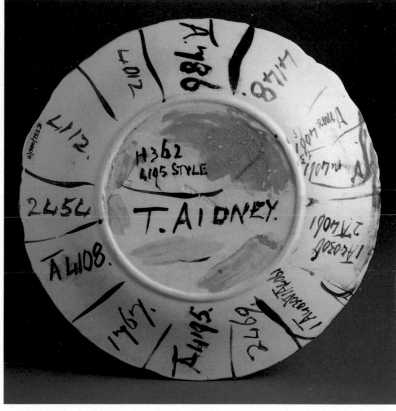

increasing use of the rich, lustrous dark green, brown and yellow glazes that had been popular on eighteenth-century creamware (Figure 117). Lacking the ability to develop glazes for themselves, small manufacturers relied upon the services of "colormakers," who specialized in developing glazes and enamel compounds and who typically did not produce ware (Figures 118 and 119). Staffordshire colormakers supplied potters worldwide and probably contributed to American majolica production. They were among a variety of established support industries that benefited significantly from the popularity of majolica and other colorful ware. Principal colormakers of the majolica period included Francis Emery and Sons of Burslem, where successes enabled expansion at Codbridge in 1877,[5] Thomas William Harrison (1843–1909), of Hanley, and Thomas Aidney and Co., active during the 1880s.

It was in the area of kiln design and improvement that Leon Arnoux made what are arguably his greatest and most frequently overlooked contributions to the Victorian ceramics industry. From his arrival at Minton's until the end of the century, Arnoux patented and perfected a series of highly efficient kilns for biscuit and glost (glaze) firing, which proved lucrative for himself and his employer and significantly increased the prestige of Minton's. By 1875, not including fourteen ovens already in use at Minton's, some thirty-five Minton's patent ovens designed by Arnoux were installed in the Staffordshire Potteries and others in the locality, including the factories of Wedgwood and Maw & Company, and many others were used on the continent by such manufacturers as Messrs. Utzschneider and Co., of the Sarreguemines factory in France (Figure 120). Of muffle type, Arnoux's kilns were designed to be espe-

Figure 118. Majolica-glaze tester plate, *above left*, of Copeland manufacture, its glazing compound produced by Thomas Aidney & Co., circa 1875. Colormakers worked on biscuit-fired blanks, supplied by their customers to test the performance and compatibility of different glazes. The enormous success of Minton's majolica was largely due to the range of compatible, opaque colored glazes developed by Leon Arnoux before 1851. Most smaller manufacturers of majolica in the Potteries purchased glazing compounds from colormakers, including Thomas Aidney & Co., which also produced enamels and all manner of raw materials for painted surface decoration. *Gladstone Pottery Museum, Longton*

Figure 119. Back of the tester plate, *above*, illustrated in Figure 118. *Gladstone Pottery Museum, Longton*

Figure 120. Sarreguemines majolica vase, *above*, patterned with arum lilies, bulrushes, and sedges, circa 1890, impressed marks, height 16¾". Vases of this large scale with profuse ornament were sold in pairs to adorn mantelpieces. The palette of colors in this example is clearly inspired by English majolica and was achieved by the use of kilns designed by Leon Arnoux. *Britannia, Gray's Antique Market, London*

Figure 121. Minton majolica jug, *above right*, in the form of a Pompeiian wine ewer, impressed marks and date code for 1870. Height 8". The library of art books available to Minton designers included numerous illustrated volumes of classical antiquities. This design is taken from a book illustrating objects recently excavated from Pompeii. *Minton Museum, Royal Doulton Ltd.*

Figure 122. Another example of the Pompeiian ewer, *right*, in smear-glazed Parian ware with celadon ground, circa 1880, height 8". All the larger manufacturers of majolica ware used their master molds, which were expensive to produce, to cast in various bodies and produce ware of various types. *Minton Museum, Royal Doulton Ltd.*

cially suitable for the production of high-glazed ware. Their advantages were outlined in promotional leaflets, such as the one presented to Wedgwood in 1875.[6]

The quantity of air thrown into the interior renders this oven perfectly *smokeless*, the carbon and the gases being so thoroughly burnt that the flues, which are intended to carry out the products of the combustion, contain only hot air, nitrogen, and carbonic acid. The superabundance of carbonic acid proves that this mode of firing is highly oxidizing, and consequently increases the richness of colours, and also the glossiness and brilliancy of glazed earthenware or china.[7]

True Majolica, Body Types and Molding Techniques

By the late 1850s, "the demand [for majolica] was increasing beyond the utmost capabilities of the vast establishments at Stoke to supply."[8] Some manufacturers found it to their commercial advantage to decorate models designed for production in Parian with majolica glazes and produce them using suitable bodies (Figures 121 and 122). Wedgwood went as far as to reintroduce designs of eighteenth-century ware glazed in majolica colors (Figures 123–125). Other, smaller Staffordshire manufacturers commonly relied on glazing readily available and traditional Staffordshire models of earlier nineteenth-century origin in the majolica technique. Thus, we can distinguish two "families" of majolica ware today: objects that were designed for general production and decorated in the majolica technique, and objects that were exclusively designed for and produced as majolica ware. It is within this latter group, the "true majolica," that the most successful items are typically found, those that best exploit the technique and represent its best intentions. In this respect, the products of smaller, specialized manufacturers of majolica, notably George Jones, who concentrated on designing and producing majolica ware, are more likely to be "true majolica" than those of the larger manufacturers, which offered a wider product range.

One great advantage to the producer of any ware covered in opaque glazes is that surface flaws in the unglazed body can be tolerated. Thus production of majolica ware was expedient and profitable, as it generated little incidence of "wasters" after its initial, or "biscuit," firing, in contrast to Parian ware, for example, which was required to be flawless, owing to its undecorated state. Most manufacturers who made both wares

charged Parian at the same price as majolica, following Minton's lead,[9] although majolica ware allowed for the use of a simple, medium-firing, unvitrified body.

Minton used a traditional, buff-colored earthenware body for the majority of their majolica, the natural color of which is visible through the transparent lead glaze put on the underside of most vessels and plates. All ceramic bodies are a mixture of alumina and silica. The Minton body consisted of alumina-rich local fire-clays in combination with gray (also called blue) clay, imported by canal and rail from the southwest of England, and silica in the form of Welsh flint that had been calcined (crushed and burnt to an ash) before mixing.[10] Similar bodies were used by most

Figure 123. Minton majolica table salt modeled as a gallant in eighteenth-century costume, date code for 1868, height 7½". This model, one of a pair including a female companion, was designed for production in the Parian body. *Collection of Mr. & Mrs. G. Leberfeld*

Figure 124. Wedgwood majolica candlestick of dolphin form, impressed marks and date code for 1867, height 9½". Many of Wedgwood's early models, including this example, which dates from the 1790s, proved highly successful when glazed in the majolica technique.

Staffordshire manufacturers, notably Brown-Westhead, Moore and Copeland's, although George Jones initially used a denser, higher-firing body for most production models, resulting in a ware of lighter weight, thinner wall, and more brittle nature.

Jones was not equipped with the technical expertise or heritage of larger, long-established potteries, and simply adopted the popular Staffordshire bodies used in the manufacture of pearlware (for most models) and ironstone ware (for larger objects) during the first half of the nineteenth century. In contrast, the Wedgwood company had a century of technical innovations and excellence in ceramic technology to draw upon when they introduced majolica-glazed ware in the early 1860s. Wedgwood employed a variety of refined bodies, including a simple buff earthenware similar to Minton's, and a dense, white earthenware that was used for most of their majolica ware and was especially suited for objects that were smaller and more intricately modeled, such as table salts and figurines. Occasionally, sculptural majolica pieces were made in Parian-type porcelain to exploit the molded detail (Figure 129). The decoration of large porcelain figural groups with majolica glazes was certainly a costly and difficult procedure, and examples made in this technique, which appears to be exclusively Wedgwood's, are extremely rare.

The heritage upon which Wedgwood, Minton, and other larger manufacturers could draw was not limited to body formulas and glaze recipes. Actual designs, in the form of molds of pattern books, were meticulously compiled, maintained, and closely guarded by Victorian potters. Designs for cast holloware, plates, and figures were kept as plaster of Paris molds, including a master (male) mold in the form of the finished object, and a working (female) mold, both of which were coated with a varnish or protective shellac. Master molds for tiles and architectural earthenware were also kept in plaster of Paris,

Figure 125. Wedgwood majolica "Triton" candlestick, *left*, (made as a pair), impressed marks and date code for 1863, height 11½". Some of Wedgwood's earliest majolica designs, including this example, were interpretations of well-known eighteenth-century models. This candlestick design was first made in the early 1770s in the black *basaltes* body. Unlike some hollow ware, which was pressed or slip-cast from original or identical molds, the majolica Triton candlesticks were remodeled in simpler and slightly taller form for majolica production (see Figure 126).

Figure 126. Wedgwood "Triton" candlesticks, *below*, in blue-and-white jasper ware, circa 1785, height 12", and in majolica, circa 1863, height 11½".

Figure 128. Wedgwood majolica bread tray, *below*, impressed marks and date code for 1878, length 13". A fine example of "true majolica" with warm, rich coloration. The tactile appeal of the relief-molded ornament is a subtle feature of good majolica and was certainly considered at the conceptual stage of design.

Figure 127. Wedgwood majolica oval dish with cauliflower pattern, *above*, impressed marks and date code for 1878, length, over handles, 13½". This model, which is most successful in majolica glaze, was made by Wedgwood in creamware in the 1760s, when the lustrous green glaze was first used. *Collection of Mr. & Mrs. G. Leberfeld*

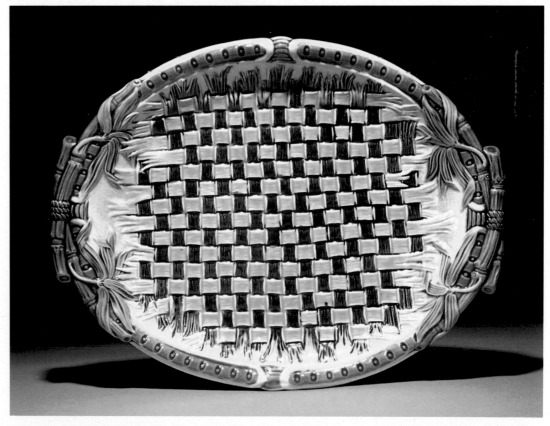

Figure 129. Maw & Company majolica tile panel, *above*, from an interior scheme, circa 1880. *Ironbridge Gorge Museum Trust*

Figure 130. Wedgwood porcelain figural group, *opposite*, of *Isaah and Rebekah*, modeled by William Beattie, circa 1862, with majolica-glazed decoration, height 17″. A rare and highly successful example of a figural group of Parian type porcelain finished in majolica glazes.

Figure 131. Group of plaster of Paris master tile molds, *above*, used by Maw & Company in the production of the panel illustrated in Figure 129. *Ironbridge Gorge Museum Trust*

and relief tile designs were sometimes cast into metal dies for use on presses (Figures 130, 131, and 132).

The art department responsible for these designs was headed by a director and included painters, modelers and other designers, most of whom worked directly from existing images[11] and found little artistic inspiration within themselves. Such practice was especially prevalent under the influence of Victorian revivalism and is still typical within the Staffordshire Potteries.

The period for majolica production saw considerable changes in the manufacturing industry of the Staffordshire potters, the results of improvements in automation and firing techniques, significant fluctuations in demand, and changing roles within the work force. The increased introduc-

tion of automation was naturally opposed by the workers, who were already organized into labor unions by mid-century. Despite the looming threat brought about by redundancy from machines, the individual skills of the makers of flatware and holloware remained fundamental to the industry throughout the nineteenth century.[12] Most majolica ware of hollow type was made by the technique of slip casting, which is still widely practiced by hand today. Throwing was largely reserved for the production of "artistic" porcelain and some simple useful wares of smaller type (Figure 133). Flatware, saucers, plates and bowls were made by a variant of the slip casting technique, whereby forms were cast as solids and pressed into shape. This technique was still subject to the workman's skills in mid-century, but hands were gradually re-

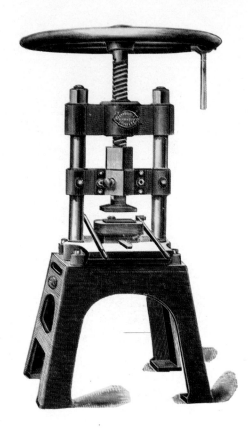

department and models for painters, most of whom were women, many in their teens.

The making of large-scale objects is a challenge potters in Staffordshire have always enjoyed. By 1851, Minton fired large objects, including majolica statuary shown at the Great Exhibition, in a kiln built expressly for the purpose,[13] and secrets of making monumental majolica were explained by a visitor to the Minton works in the mid-1880s: "The big work . . . storks and cranes and peacocks are very often molded or cast in several pieces which are afterwards bound together before they are dry and are submitted to the kiln. The various sections are united by a thin roll or bank of slip, no sign of which is permitted to appear, and perfect cohesion is ensured by all being fixed together."[14] Majolica ware, with all surfaces covered in thick, opaque glaze, was especially suitable for the manufacture of large-scale objects, a market which Minton fully exploited (Figure 134).

Figure 132. A hand-operated vertical tile press, *far left*, of pillar type by W. Boulton of Burslem. *Ironbridge Gorge Museum Trust*

placed by automatic templates called "jolleys" and, later, "jiggers," especially during the 1870s.

Each stage of majolica production was carried out in an area specifically designed for the purpose by specially trained workers. At Minton's, for example, a number of innovations were introduced into the conventional production system that took an object from conception in the art department to realization in the kiln. Following the approval of working drawings by the art director (usually Leon Arnoux), the design was modeled in plaster of Paris in the model-making shop in the conventional manner. Then several master blanks were cast and painted in a palette resembling majolica glazes. In this state, the master models were stored and (by about 1875) photographed for a design record index from which designs for production could ultimately be selected. Painted molds also served as proofs for the art

Figure 133. A Minton thrower at work, *left*, circa 1900. Throwing at Minton was reserved for the production of porcelain and, later, for artistic earthenwares: all majolica holloware was made by the slip-casting process. Notice the pocket watch hanging within sight of the potter, evidence of the strict schedules to which workers in the industry still conform. *Minton Museum, Royal Doulton Ltd.*

Figure 135. Meissen porcelain heron, *below*, of life size, modeled by Johann Joachim Kaendler (1706–1775), circa 1731. Kaendler produced a number of highly animated, full-scale animal figures in porcelain at the Meissen works in the 1730s, using stuffed animals as models. He even attempted a life-size equestrian statue of Augustus III, but it was never completed. There is no doubt that the remarkable works of Kaendler and his contemporaries were the principal sources of inspiration for the large animal and bird sculptures produced by Minton and others a century and a half later.

Figure 134. Minton majolica figure of a stork, *above*, modeled by John Henk, date code for 1875, height 44″. The large-scale and life-size animal figures, many of which were modeled by John Henk and Paul Colomera between 1870 and 1885, are among the most technically and artistically advanced in the Minton majolica range. Typically, while figures of similar type produced by other manufacturers were designed to function as large vases or umbrella stands, Minton's examples were intended exclusively as decorative ceramic sculpture. This tradition was inherited from porcelain modelers at the Meissen works in the early eighteenth century, as was the technique of incorporating smaller creatures, such as the unfortunate snake and frog in this model, into the assemblage. *Minton Museum, Royal Doulton Ltd.*

4

English Majolica Manufacturers and Their Marks

For thirty years
nothing was more popular than
Minton's majolica, whether for
ornamental ware, tiles or facades.

Josiah C. Wedgwood

Figure 136. Design for a border, *above*, to be molded in relief and painted in majolica colors, probably drawn by Thomas Kirkby; annotations by Leon Arnoux include suggestions for additional florettes. *Minton Museum, Royal Doulton Ltd.*

Figure 137. Minton majolica plate in Renaissance taste, *opposite*, made for the Crystal Palace Art Union, 1860, impressed facsimile signature mark, diameter 10½". The English Art Union Movement was founded in the late 1830s as part of the general movement toward reform in art and design. Founded in 1858, the Crystal Palace Art Union was one of the largest; it was renamed The Ceramic and Crystal Palace Art Union in 1865. Most of the objects the Union commissioned and promoted were Parian sculpture, but a few examples of majolica ware are also recorded. *Collection of Mr. & Mrs. G. Leberfeld*

M  inton   The Minton Porcelain Manufacturing Company was founded in 1793 by Thomas Minton (1765–1836), a native of Shropshire, and continued as a family business until 1968, when it became a member of the Royal Doulton Tableware Group. During most of the first half of the nineteenth century, the boom period in English porcelain manufacture, Minton developed a reputation as a maker of earthenware and porcelain of the highest quality, relying for its success on progressive design and superior technical ability. Thomas Minton was succeeded by his son, Herbert, following his death in 1836. By this time, the Minton family had successfully acquired a considerable collection of "old porcelains," notably eighteenth-century ware from the Sèvres factory in France and *Kangxi* wares from China. Objects from this collection, including the more impressive Sèvres porcelain vases, some of which were borrowed from other collections for this purpose, were copied by or served as inspiration to the Minton designers and technicians. Reproductions, revivals, or facsimiles, albeit of superb technical execution, dominated output under Herbert Minton's early administration. By midcentury, public taste called for more sophisticated and innovative designs, and from his appointment as art director in 1849, Leon Arnoux began to meet demand by introducing new products, materials, techniques, and original designs for shapes and decoration of ware. Arnoux was particularly active in the traditional capacity of art director during the 1850s, when all designs for the new majolica line were subject to his approval.[2] Arnoux's supervisory role can be identified in many of the original working drawings from the 1850s that are preserved in the Minton archives and which include notations, suggestions, and alterations in his hand (Figure 137).

During the early years of majolica production, Arnoux's principal designer at Minton was

Figure 138. Parian commemorative figure of Colin Minton Campbell, *above*, modeled by Thomas Longmore in May 1887. *Minton Museum, Royal Doulton Ltd.*

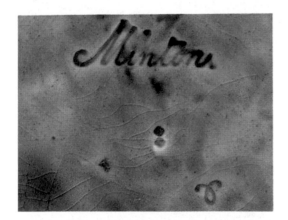

Figure 139. Impressed facsimile signature mark, *above*, on the back of the Art Union plate illustrated in Figure 137. The impressed cipher below indicates production in 1860. *Collection of Mr. & Mrs. G. Leberfeld*

Figure 140. Minton majolica figural table salt, *above right*, impressed marks and date code for 1863, height 7¾". A good example of Minton's elaborate table ornaments, which were typically sold in pairs. *Britannia, Gray's Antique Market, London*

Thomas Kirkby (1824–1890), who joined Minton's in 1845 and worked there until 1887, when failing health forced his retirement. Kirkby is best known for his authentic reproductions, produced under Arnoux's guidance, of sixteenth-century Italian earthenwares, some made under the auspices of art unions (Figure 138). Kirkby and his colleagues relied for their sources of inspiration on existing historical objects, including examples from the Minton family collection as well as Italian *maiolica* and Palissy ware from the Louvre and South Kensington museums, copied from book illustrations and the occasional borrowed object. These designs fall into the early range of Minton's majolica design numbers, with the prefix G[3] that included, by the spring of 1853, garden stools (ten models), bread trays, door plates, bowls, vases, jardinieres, flower baskets, candlesticks, inkwells, pedestals, girandoles for wall mounting, doorknobs, and a variety of objects for table and desk usage.[4] By

the early 1860s, sculptural majolica proliferated, some examples of which were majolica-glazed earthenware cast in molds designed for Parian production (Figure 140).

It is generally accepted that the Great Exhibition of 1851 was the debut forum for Minton's majolica ware, and there is little evidence to dispute this. Designs for "majolica" appear in Minton pattern books as early as 1849.[5] Production ware with this trademark was probably on sale before the summer of 1851, but the Exhibition clearly presented a unique opportunity to officially introduce a "new line," and several designs were made expressly for it,[6] including sculptural vases modeled by Albert Carrier and a variety of large jardinieres suitable for conservatories.

Anyone who has ever participated in a commercial exhibition will be familiar with the chaos that immediately precedes a public opening. The Great Exhibition of the Industry of All Nations

Figure 141. Two Minton majolica match holders (not a pair), *left*, modeled as a basket holder and a washer woman, circa 1870; height of the taller is 9½". *Collection of Mr. & Mrs. G. Leberfeld*

Figure 142. Minton majolica figural spill vase, *above*, modeled by John Henk, impressed marks and date code for 1876, height 13". The figural majolica modeled by Henk, some of which bears an incised signature, as on this example, was among the company's finest products. *Britannia, Gray's Antique Market, London*

was no exception. At the age of 23, Colin Minton Campbell (1827–1885) was responsible for supervising the set-up of his company's stand (the arrangement of which was designed by Leon Arnoux), and wrote enthusiastically of the confusion to his mother:

> Even until the last we were constantly annoyed and disturbed by workmen over 2,000 of whom toiled around the clock with scaffolds, paint pots and tools to ready the Hall and its exhibition stands. We were visited by a great many people while so engaged and had the honor of escorting the Duke of Devonshire, Duchess of Sutherland and others. Prince Albert (accompanied by the Princess of Prussia) also came twice and the Queen once.[7]

Colin Minton Campbell appeared to feel the customary awe of a provincial Englishman toward nobility. He did have the opportunity to speak with Prince Albert and Queen Victoria,[8] though the principal job of escorting notables was left to Herbert Minton, no stranger to upper social circles. Minton, known to the royal family as "that manufacturer of beautiful dessert services," had the honor of escorting Queen Victoria, Prince Albert, and the Prince and Princess of Prussia through the entire exhibition—before the public opening, of course. Colin Minton Campbell remarked that Minton's efforts deserved "nothing short of a place in the peerage," an honor which was never bestowed.

Despite the chaos during the set-up, which was probably not alleviated by the visitation of hordes of nobility and dignitaries which required Herbert Minton to "move from one place to another with the speed of the electric telegraph,"[9] the exhibition opened in glorious circumstances and without a hitch. Many present remarked upon

Figure 144. Minton majolica cream jug, *below*, in the form of a frog squatting on an eggplant, impressed marks and date code for 1872, height 4″. One of the most noticeable influences of *Japonisme* was the introduction to Western designers of an entirely new repertoire of art motifs, two of which are skillfully combined in this design. *Collection of Dr. & Mrs. Denny B. Lotwin*

Figure 143. Minton monochrome glazed jug, *above*, of pineapple form, 1881, height 9″. This example can correctly be considered majolica ware and is sometimes found naturalistically colored in yellow and green glazes. *Collection of Dr. & Mrs. Howard Silby*

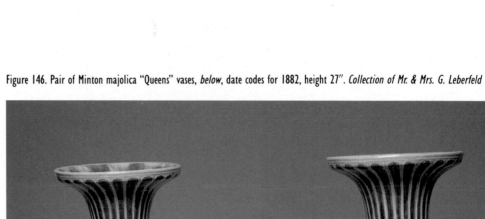

Figure 146. Pair of Minton majolica "Queens" vases, *below*, date codes for 1882, height 27″. *Collection of Mr. & Mrs. G. Leberfeld*

Figure 145. Minton majolica wine cradle, *above*, designed circa 1875, length 13″. *Collection of Joan Esch; photograph by Gary Samson*

Figure 148. Minton majolica footed nautilus shell bowl, *below*, impressed marks and date code for 1862, height 9¼". *Britannia, Gray's Antique Market, London*

the silence which filled the hall during the ceremonial entrance of Queen Victoria in the presence of 30,000 loyal subjects who watched "without a single insult."[10] The silence was partially achieved by the strategic assignment of falconeers to remove a large number of finches and other songbirds from the hall immediately before the opening ceremonies. Colin Minton Campbell enthusiastically dubbed the opening ceremony "certainly the proudest day that England ever witnessed."[11]

Minton's majolica received one of only two Special Council Medals awarded at the Great Exhibition for "originality and beauty of design," a compliment which could justifiably be paid to the majority of majolica designs produced by Minton over the next four decades.

Throughout the majolica period, Minton pursued a policy of engaging and encouraging both young and established British and foreign designers to exploit their unique abilities in the spirit of what Herbert Minton termed "mutual coopera-

tion and friendly feeling,"[12] an important legacy to British industry from the Great Exhibition. The production of majolica ware, which proved to be among Minton's most successful contributions in 1851, profitted especially well from the influx of foreign talent. Many of the imported workers were modelers, notably Albert Carrier, who continued his relationship with Minton sporadically for thirty years following his cessation of permanent employment in 1855. Working from his Paris studio, in Rue de la Tour d'Auvergne, he submitted designs to Minton for approval in the form of plaster casts, paid for on a royalty basis. Carrier achieved considerable prominence in French academic and ceramic circles.[13] He was admired by Napoleon III, who referred to him as "our Clodion,"[14] and his later correspondence with Minton suggests that he considered employment somewhat beneath him, a factor that may have contributed to his return to France after only six years in the Potteries. He expressed such dissatisfaction in a letter to Colin Minton Campbell in 1882:

Your personal taste and manufacturing methods could sometimes be the obstacles to an otherwise perfect relationship between us.[15]

Not all Minton artists who worked on staff or on commission shared this outlook, however, and most had unfailing respect for their employer. Other artists of note not previously mentioned who contributed to majolica design included Alfred Stevens, a London sculptor who worked between 1859 and 1861; George Leason, a modeler who designed several oyster plates; Edmund G. Reuter, who designed architectural majolica and tiles from 1875 until about 1895; Eugene Phoenix, a modeler; Thomas Longmore, a gifted modeler who worked mainly in Parian between 1870 and 1898; and Christian Henk, a German modeler who came from Coburg in 1851 and, together with his son John Henk (1863–1914), was responsible for many of Minton's later figural majolica of monumental scale, including some of the famous peacock figures.

The Great Exhibition was not the first international event in which Minton had participated, but the enormous success which the company derived from it gave them the encouragement to exhibit frequently at international fairs for the rest of the century. This policy was strongly pursued by Colin Minton Campbell, who became so well acquainted with these events that he was invited to serve on a General Purposes Committee for London International Exhibitions, some twenty-one years after his enthusiastic contribution at the Crystal Palace. Campbell's advice on these matters was politely sought by other manufacturers, notably the Wedgwood Company.[16] Under his guidance, Minton participated in over a dozen exhibitions until Campbell's death in 1885.

Minton's display at the London International Exhibition of 1862 was magnificent. The exhibition hall was an elongated glass-roofed structure that featured a fountain in majolica ware crowned

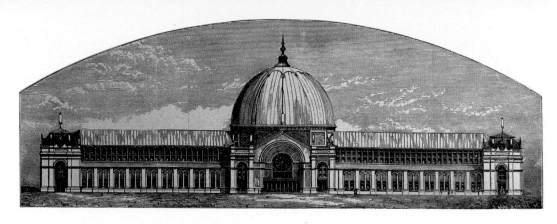

Figure 149. Front elevation of the main Exhibition building, London, 1862.

Figure 150. The magnificent "St. George and the Dragon" majolica fountain that was displayed at the London Exhibition of 1862, from a contemporary stereoscopic view. Thirty-six feet in height, the imposing structure was modeled by John Thomas, who also sculpted in Parian for Minton, notably the well-known "Lady Godiva" figure. *Minton Museum, Royal Doulton Ltd.*

with a larger-than-life size figure of "St. George Slaying the Dragon" installed under the dome at the terminal of the Hall's eastern wing (Figure 150). The fountain, which stood over thirty-six feet high and measured thirty-nine feet at the diameter of its base, was designed by John Thomas, a London sculptor who died before its installation, and was praised by contemporary critics as "a magnificent triumph of the potter's art."[17] The exhibition of 1862 included a large majolica contingent from Minton, including vases designed by William Goode and sculptural majolica modeled by Albert Carrier, and was one of several influential post–Great Exhibition events in England in which Minton participated before the end of the century, notably the South Kensington Exhibition in 1871.

Paris, bolstered by enormous state financial support and a desire to re-establish France as the international center of new design, hosted two universal exhibitions in the 1850s (1853 and 1855) where Minton successfully showed majolica ware. The first of the truly large-scale Parisian universal exhibitions was held in 1867, providing the model for the highly successful Paris exhibitions of 1889 (for which the Eiffel Tower was built), and 1900 (for which the Grand Palais was built).

Majolica ware was greatly in evidence in Paris in 1867. Minton's, with the promotional assistance of Thomas Goode & Company, their London retailer and agent, populated the entire site with garden stools, flower pots, and an assortment of other items, and presented an enormous stand crowned with "works of cost and magnitude,"[18] but also included "the varied objects that all housekeepers require,"[19] in an attempt to cultivate the expanding international market for domestic ceramics. Minton enjoyed further successes at the Paris Exhibition of 1878, for which Colin Minton Campbell was awarded the *Legion d'Honneur*, and at the Exhibition of 1889 that featured the famous pair of monumental earthenware elephants, which are more than seven feet in height and

Figure 151. An impressive Minton majolica plant stand in the form of a female blackamoor, the modeling attributed to Albert Carrier, circa 1862. *Minton Museum, Royal Doulton Ltd.*

now grace Thomas Goode's London store.

During the 1870s, the popularity of international exhibitions increased, and manufacturers of majolica exploited such events to promote their new designs and introduce their products to a wider market. Minton maintained a stock of impressive exhibition pieces which traveled around the world for this promotional function (Figure 152).[20] At the Vienna Exhibition of 1873, majolica from Staffordshire dominated the decorative ceramics exhibits with a display of Minton ware taking pride of place in the center of the central aisle. The company showed very successfully, taking home only sixty-four items from a stock of 549.[21]

Other international exhibitions during the 1870s in which Minton participated included the United States Centennial Exhibition, held in Philadelphia in 1876, and one in Sydney, Australia in 1879. While geographical and demographical diversity of the host cities allowed exhibitors to take advantage of varying conditions of demand, these factors also served to create confusion. In Philadelphia, for instance, majolica from Staffordshire and the Continent was eagerly received by an affluent American public that was keen to imitate what they perceived to be the sophisticated tastes of Europe and to consume modern decorative arts. Two years later, however, in Paris, where the progressive stirrings of the Art Nouveau movement were just beginning to be felt and the enlightening influence of *Japonisme* was turning modern design into a new direction, majolica was less in evidence and manufacturers were beginning to sense a decline in demand (see page 108).

By the mid-1870s, Minton was among the largest manufacturers of decorative ceramics in the world with over 1,500 employees, more than 200 of whom were earthenware enamelers, principally employed in majolica production.[22] Despite high production costs imposed by laborious hand decoration and the great expense of new molds,[23] the company produced an enormous selection of

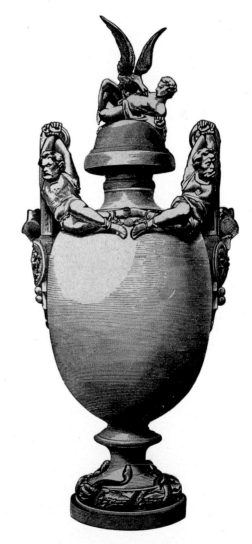

Figure 152. A monumental Minton majolica and enamel-painted "Prometheus" vase, *left*, modeled by Victor Simeon and painted in the manner of Edward Rischgitz, impressed marks and date code for 1870, height 4′ 1½″. At least six examples of the "Prometheus" vase were manufactured, but this is the only recorded example with polychrome figure painting. Majolica of this scale and standard was made for prestigious display at international exhibitions and was kept in stock by Minton's agents for this purpose. *Author's Collection: Photo; Sotheby's, New York*

Figure 153. A majolica-glazed but undecorated example of Minton's "Prometheus" vase, *above*, exhibited in Philadelphia in 1876. The vase was probably modeled in 1866 and first displayed at the Paris Exposition in the following year.

Figure 154. Majolica clock with thermometer/barometer case, exhibited at the Philadelphia Centennial Exhibition of 1876, approximate height 24″. This remarkable object, attributed to Minton's, was praised by contemporary critics for its "richness and brilliancy." The ground color was turquoise applied with "chocolates, greens, yellows, and flesh tones." The excessive use of Renaissance Revival ornament is typical of English products aimed at the wealthier American patron. English majolica of superior quality was in great evidence at the Philadelphia Centennial Exhibition of 1876, where Minton's was represented by the London retailer Daniell and Son.

majolica ware ranging from humble table articles to gigantic fountains. Minton was also responsible for vast quantities of majolica tiling and architectural ornament, most of which was made under the direction of Michael Daintry Hollins, a nephew of Herbert Minton by marriage, who went into partnership with him in 1845. A year after Herbert Minton's death in 1859, Hollins assumed full control of the tile business, which was then carried on at a wholly separate, adjacent works, using the name Minton Hollins & Co. (Figure 155). By 1870, majolica tiles were also made by Colin Minton Campbell, who traded in that capacity as the Campbell Brick & Tile Company.

Colin Minton Campbell died in 1885, and production at the Minton factory declined steadily for the next ten years, during which time earthenware turnover showed consistently at a loss.[24] In 1892, in failing health, Leon Arnoux retired, relinquishing the position of art director he had held for over forty years to his grandson, Leon Solon. Production of majolica dwindled during the 1890s as public taste in pottery swung toward "art wares" and the more progressive styles of Continental Europe and the English Arts and Crafts Movement, which finally achieved respectability under the promotional guidance of Sir Arthur Lazenby Liberty, the founder of Liberty's of Regent Street.

Figure 155. Minton majolica butter dish cover, and stand, *above*, impressed marks, circa 1865, diameter of stand 9″. *Collection of Joan Esch; photograph by Gary Samson*

Figure 156. A majolica-glazed wall tile, *left*, circa 1870, including a monogram letter H for Michael Daintry Hollins, removed from Minton Hollins showroom at Shelton Road, Stoke-on-Trent. *Gladstone Pottery Museum, Longton*

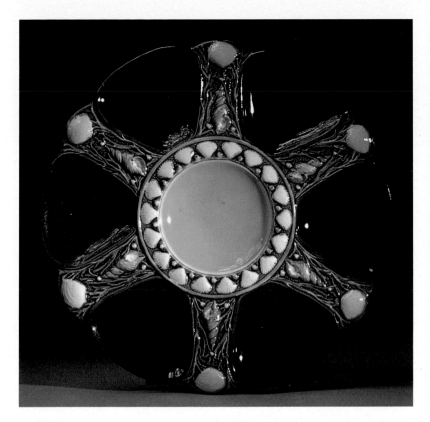

Figure 157. Minton majolica oyster plate, *above*, 1874, diameter 9″. A typical example of Minton's oyster plates in formal taste. *Collection of Dr. & Mrs. Howard Silby*

Figure 158. The back of the oyster plate, *above right*, in figure 157. Minton wares often include a profusion of marks. Note the registry mark, which indicates the date (month and year) that the design of this model was registered; the cipher, indicating the year of production; and the painted batch mark within the unglazed area, a technique learned by George Jones and often used on his products. *Collection of Dr. & Mrs. Howard Silby*

Following Arnoux's departure, his majolica glazes were applied to various Minton "Art" lines, most successfully to "Secessionist" ware, which derived its ornamental inspiration from the unique style of the Vienna Secession School, formed in the mid-1890s.

Majolica ware's decline was augmented by changing patterns in social custom and urban dwelling that restricted the demand for much of the specialized majolica which had been so popular among the previous generation. Some pressure to restrict or modify majolica glazes was provided from government statutes of the late 1890s concerning the lead content of glazes, but changes in taste were the principal reason for its disappearance. The last recorded public display of Minton majolica was in 1894, when a few examples[25] were shown at the Imperial Institute Exhibition of Pottery and Glass in London.

Leon Arnoux died in 1902, a few months after

the bulk of the Minton family collection of Minton ceramics and "old porcelains" was dispersed by Christie's at their King Street Rooms.[26] By the time of his death, the majolica Arnoux had invented was already considered *declassé* by a public infused with the optimism of a new century which promised to break free from the artistic bonds of revivalism.

The vast majority of Minton majolica is marked. From 1842, the company impressed date ciphers (a table of which is reproduced here) which indicate the year of potting only. Thus, ciphers cannot be used to date a design's origin. Year ciphers are usually accompanied by an impressed capital letter indicating the month of potting; a personal potter's mark may also appear as a letter. In 1862, the company began impressing the name MINTON on all earthenwares, and this became MINTONS ten years later. Registry marks are not uncommon on Minton majolica.

T able
of
Minton
Datemarks

1850	1851	1852	1853	1854	1855	1856	1857
♣	∴	V	⌒	ʕ	✳	♀	◇
1858	1859	1860	1861	1862	1863	1864	1865
⋔	Ⅱ	♌	⅄	⚲	◈	Z	≋
1866	1867	1868	1869	1870	1871	1872	1873
X	X	G	⊡	Ⓜ	Ⓝ	⊗	✳
1874	1875	1876	1877	1878	1879	1880	1881
↓	Ɛ	◬	◑	△	△	△	⊞
1882	1883	1884	1885	1886	1887	1888	1889
⊗	⊘	⊠	⋈	B	♔	∞	S
1890	1891	1892	1893	1894	1895	1896	1897
T	⛨	⛨	⛨	⛨	🦆	🦆	🦆

The name of Wedgwood is probably the best known and most highly respected in the history of English ceramics. The company, which continues to thrive in Staffordshire today, was established in the mid-eighteenth century by Josiah Wedgwood I, who set a precedent of excellence in ceramic technique, design, and marketing which remains unparalleled. In the mid-nineteenth century, the business based at the Etruria Works was continued by Francis Wedgwood, grandson of Josiah I, and he was joined by his three sons during the 1860s. The eldest son, Godfrey Wedgwood, who served as art director for most of his tenure, was chiefly responsible for the revival which the Wedgwood company experienced in the 1860s, as attention was increasingly turned toward the development of new and innovative products and higher standards of manufacture and design. The new types of ware introduced under the guidance of Godfrey Wedgwood included Parian, glazed tiles, a variety of "artistic wares" painted and modeled by prominent artists, "Email Ombrant," described below, and majolica.

Despite the enormous success that Minton had exhibited with majolica, Wedgwood was slow to introduce their own line. This was partly due to the company's resistance to experimental work during its economic recovery in the 1850s[27] and the range of majolica-type green- and brown-glazed ware that had been in successful production since the mid-eighteenth century (Figures 159 and 160). The first evidence of Wedgwood majolica appeared in May 1862, by which time Wedgwood was flourishing and enjoying what Meteyard called the "Staffordshire Renaissance" of that year,[28] when Godfrey Wedgwood sought the advice of Colin Minton Campbell on majolica pricing.[29] From the beginning, Wedgwood followed the example of Minton in majolica production and promotion. A number of prominent Minton designers and modelers were

Figure 159. Wedgwood majolica "Doric" jug, *right*, in mottled green and brown reduction glazes, impressed marks and date code for 1869, height 8½". *Collection of Mr. & Mrs. G. Leberfeld*

Figure 160. Wedgwood majolica sideplate, *below*, in the "Stanley" pattern, impressed marks and date code for 1869, diameter 7¾". Throughout the majolica period, Wedgwood continued a technique that had been introduced in the 1750s, applying mottled glazes to create a "tortoise-shell" effect. *Collection of Dr. & Mrs. Howard Silby*

Figure 161. Wedgwood majolica centerpiece, *left*, modeled in the manner of Hughes Protat, impressed marks and date code for 1867, height 13". Large table centerpieces such as this were most impressive when overflowing with fruit; the shell-form dishes near the base were intended to hold sweetmeats.

Figure 162. Wedgwood majolica crocus pot, *above*, in Anglo-French taste, impressed marks and date code for 1870, length 7½". This unusual object combines influences from a Baroque, Renaissance, and neoclassical past in the incongruous, agglomerated revivalist style, that was especially popular in the United States during the 1870s.

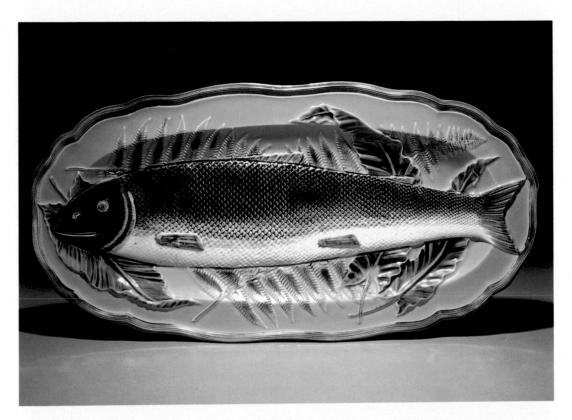

Figure 163. Wedgwood majolica salmon platter, *left*, impressed marks and date code for 1877, length 25″.

Figure 164. Wedgwood majolica plaque, *below*, in the form of a salmon, impressed marks and date code for 1878, length 22½″. This enigmatic object, cast from the center of the mold used in the making of the salmon platter illustrated in Figure 163, is pierced with two holes at the top and was presumably intended to be hung as a wall decoration or trade sign.

employed, including Albert Carrier and Hughes Protat, both of whom designed for Wedgwood on a free-lance basis, and there is little difference between the Anglo-French–style ware of either company (Figures 161 and 162). By 1875, Wedgwood acknowledged the superiority of Minton's techniques by installing eight patent kilns of Leon Arnoux design at Etruria. Comprising the largest single order of the ovens to date, these proved consistently effective in producing a smooth, lustrous glaze. Wedgwood's majolica designs were not all derived from Minton, however. By 1880, the company offered a range of over 350 "fancy articles" in majolica,[30] including such diverse products as ice plates, spitting pots, and a variety of specialized table items, many of innovative and whimsical form.

Wedgwood excelled in the design and manufacture of useful ware in majolica, a market in which they were virtually unrivaled. Although the company drew upon its vast historical design resources for majolica ware (Figures 175, 176, and 177), many examples of the best Victorian "true majolica" were conceived and produced at Wedgwood, especially during the most intense period of production between about 1870 and 1880 (Figures 178 and 179).

Figure 165. Pair of Wedgwood majolica flower holders, *above*, impressed marks and date code for 1866, height 7". Small flower holders of elaborate design were intended for table usage, a function further evidenced by the small receptacles for salt incorporated into each model.

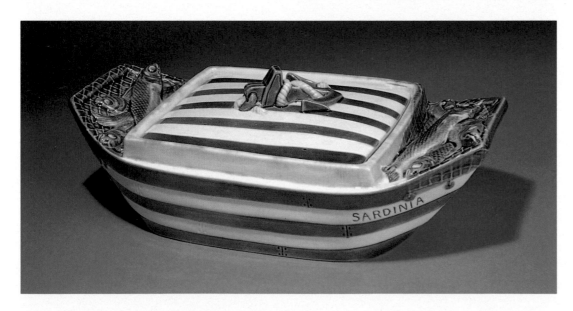

Figure 166. Wedgwood majolica sardine box, *left*, in the "Sardinia" pattern, impressed mark and registry mark for 1878, length 9¾".

Figure 167. Two Wedgwood majolica sauceboats, *above*, of nautilus shell form, impressed marks and date code for 1876, length 8″. Wedgwood offered one "spoon holder" in the majolica catalog of 1876, and this may be the design, although it was more likely intended for the serving of horseradish sauce.

Figure 168. Wedgwood majolica salt or trinket holder, *left*, in the form of a bird's nest, impressed marks and date code for 1876, height 3½″.

Figure 169. Wedgwood majolica cigar tray in the "Net" pattern, impressed marks and date code for 1870, the design registered in 1869, length 8″.

Figure 170. Wedgwood majolica ring tray, impressed marks and date code for 1876, length 6¼″.

Figure 171. Covered trinket box in Wedgwood majolica in the form of reclining neoclassical boy, impressed marks and date code for 1871, length 4¼″. A rare majolica version of the popular model known as "Somnus" that Wedgwood had produced as a letter weight in *basaltes* and other ware in the late eighteenth century.

Majolica

Figure 172. Wedgwood majolica figure of a putto with a goat, *above*, impressed marks and date code for 1868, height 9″. Nonfunctional figures and groups in Wedgwood majolica are unusual, and only six such designs were offered in the range. This model is more commonly found functioning as a spill vase with open basket.

Figure 173. Pair of Wedgwood majolica candlesticks, *below*, in the "Satyr" pattern, impressed marks and date code for 1871, height 10″. The natural white color of the earthenware body used in much of Wedgwood's majolica was especially suitable for a flesh ground and was sometimes termed "ivory finish."

Figure 174. Pair of Wedgwood majolica spill vases, *above*, modeled as a "Scotch Fisherman and Wife," impressed marks and date code for 1872, height 11″.

Figure 175. Wedgwood majolica pierced cover bowl or "chestnut basket," *opposite*, impressed marks and date code for 1862, height 8½". Wedgwood drew upon its unparalleled design resources to reproduce in the majolica technique. This model was first produced in creamware in the 1770s, when it was typically undecorated, and was manufactured in caneware later in the eighteenth century. The subtly English Rococo design was no doubt chosen to appeal to the followers of Rococo Revivalism in the 1860s.

Figure 176. Wedgwood majolica oval dish, *below*, with grape leaf pattern, 1879, length 11½". Offered under the majolica denomination as the "Grape" bread tray, in this and a smaller size, this model was first produced by Wedgwood in creamware in the 1760s. *Collection of Lloyd J. Bleier*

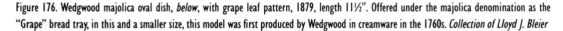

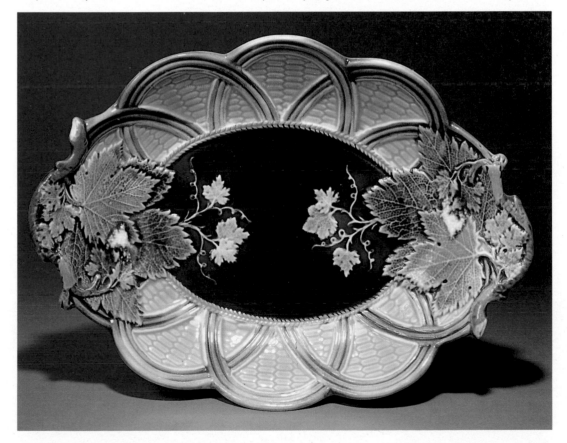

Figure 177. Wedgwood majolica double dolphin centerpiece, *above*, with nautilus top, impressed marks and date code for 1870, height 16". Another revived eighteenth-century model, this successful design was offered in majolica in two sizes, this being the larger.

Figure 178. Wedgwood majolica "Naiad" centerpiece, impressed marks, circa 1868, length 17½". One of Wedgwood's earliest majolica designs and a superb example of "true majolica," in which the naiads evoke the solemn beauty celebrated by the English pre-Raphaelite movement.

Figure 179. Wedgwood majolica jardiniere, impressed marks and date code for 1869, diameter 20″. Large, impressive hothouse ornaments of this type, some after designs by Albert Carrier, were exhibited with great success by Wedgwood at the Paris Exposition of 1867.

Figure 180. Wedgwood majolica frieze tile, *above*, modeled in relief with a neoclassical scene after Clodion, impressed marks and date code for 1866, 8″ × 13½″. Large, slab-molded majolica tiles of this type were difficult to manufacture and are rare. They were intended to be used as interior architectural ornament, and the backs are typically frogged to receive mortar.

Figure 181. Wedgwood majolica border tile, *left*, in the "Grape" pattern, impressed marks and date code for 1877, 7½″ × 7½″. Glazed on both sides, decorative tiles of this type were commonly slotted into square metal mounts to function as cachepôts (also called mignonette boxes) and were not suitable for mounting on walls.

Figure 182. Wedgwood majolica oval centerpiece, modeled in the form of two mythical "sea horses," impressed marks and date code for 1871, height 8½".

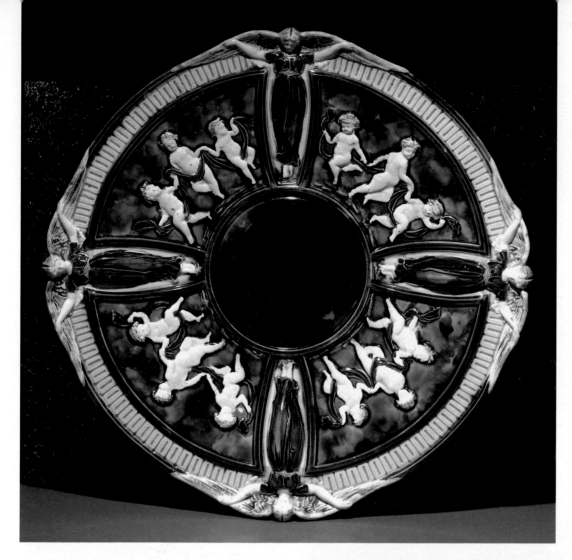

Figure 184. Wedgwood majolica butter dish and cover, *below*, in the "Stanley" pattern, impressed marks and date code for 1871, diameter 6½". This high-quality design is the work of Frederick Bret Russel, who also designed the famous "Caterer" jug (see Figure 87), along with several other works for Wedgwood, in the late 1860s. This design was registered in 1867, and the modeling is attributed to Simon Birks.

Figure 185. Wedgwood majolica allegorical figure of Autumn, *opposite*, modeled in spirited Romantic taste, impressed marks, circa 1876, height 16".

Figure 183. Wedgwood majolica cake stand, *above*, patterned with angels and putti, impressed marks and date code for 1865, diameter 12". This successful design, executed in majolica glazes on a mottled-glaze ground, combines the formal grace of the English Arts and Crafts taste with the extravagance of Rococo Revivalism.

Throughout the majolica period, however, the policy of the Wedgwood Company was to concentrate commercial production on the range of refined stonewares, notably the black "Basaltes" variety and the famous blue "Jasper" ware (known generically as Wedgwood ware) developed by Josiah Wedgwood I in the eighteenth century. Majolica ware was included in increasing but limited proportions on the Wedgwood stands at international exhibitions in the 1870s and 1880s.

The Paris Exhibition of 1878 included the usual roster of English exhibitors, including Wedgwood, Minton's, Maw & Company and Brown-Westhead, Moore. According to Charles Bachhoffner, Wedgwood's London agent and representative at that event, it was remarkable how little majolica was to be found in either the English or foreign collections; it was found in abundance only at the stand of Brown-Westhead, Moore, which, Bachhoffner speculated, was targeting the American market. This exhibition prompted Bachhoffner to suggest to Godfrey Wedgwood that "any new shapes and designs that we may bring out should be decorated otherwise than majolica finish, or else otherwise bringing them out in majolica we shall get them disliked at starting and then when we have to turn to other decoration, the novelty will be lost."[31] Bachhoffner identified the newly introduced Continental ware, which dominated stands in the French court at the exhibitions called *faience artistique*, a revived and characteristically French form of hand-painted tin-glazed earthenware, as well as *pâte-sur-pâte* and *barbotine* ware, an earthenware decorated by hand in colored slips in a technique resembling the thick *impasto* favored by some contemporary oil painters.

Despite Bachhoffner's contention that "majolica has had its day,"[32] however, production continued in Staffordshire until the end of the century, though it dwindled significantly by the mid-1880s.

The Wedgwood Company responded to the new trend by introducing a variety of majolica-

Figure 186. Wedgwood majolica dessert plate patterned with basket weave, impressed marks and date code for 1868, diameter 8¾". *Collection of Mr. & Mrs. G. Leberfeld*

glazed ware termed "Argenta," in which the natural off-white body color is left exposed as a ground and majolica glazes are applied to the cast relief ornament, typically of sparse and formalized type, in keeping with the taste for *Japonisme* and the Aesthetic style of the late 1870s (Figures 187, 188, and 189).

In 1863, Wedgwood began to experiment with a decorating technique that produced a perspective effect by filling shallow relief ornament with translucent majolica glazes.[33] This process, known as Email Ombrant (a variation of the lithophanie), had been developed by Baron du Tremblay in France in the 1840s, and examples of his work were shown in 1851 at the Great Exhibition.

Wedgwood's success with the technique was limited, and little Email Ombrant ware was produced until 1872, when the Wedgwood Company purchased all the molds,[34] designs, and glaze recipes, together with the original patent, from the Baron's estate. Ware decorated with a combination of this technique and Wedgwood's majolica glazes proliferated over the next fifteen years,

mostly in the form of ornamental or dessert plates (Figure 191).

Unlike most of their competitors, Wedgwood continued to produce majolica ware well into the interwar period of the twentieth century, and the perennial monochrome green-glazed ware is still in commercial production.

Throughout its history, the Wedgwood Company has stringently marked its wares, a policy that was closely adhered to during the majolica period. Virtually all Wedgwood majolica bears the impressed firm name in capital letters, which is supplemented with the word "ENGLAND," on pieces made after about 1892, and "MADE IN ENGLAND" on pieces made after about 1911. Pattern numbers that refer to a consecutive design index often appear on Wedgwood majolica painted underglaze, and these may include a letter prefix, which identifies the variety of ware.[35] The letter M was used on majolica from 1873 to 1888, when it was replaced by K; this was used until about 1920. From about 1884, tiles with majolica glaze use the letter prefix Q. In 1860, Wedgwood initiated a system of impressed date letters, a practice that continued until 1929. The three capital letters impressed on most Wedgwood majolica can be read to reveal the month and year of actual production (not the year the design was first introduced), using the code system explained below:

> The first letter indicates the month, the second (middle) code letter is a potter's mark, and the third shows the year of production, starting with O, in 1860. The alphabet was used in three cycles, starting with A in 1872 and again in 1898. There is potential confusion between pieces made in the third cycle with those in the second bearing the same date letter. Until 1907, when a number replaced the impressed month letter, the letter sequences can be the same despite the twenty-six-year difference.

Figure 187. Wedgwood majolica (Argenta ware) sandwich plate, *left*, impressed marks and date code for 1880, 7″×7″. *Collection of Dr. & Mrs. Denny B. Lotwin*

Figure 188. "Dragon" tea kettle, *below left*, in Wedgwood majolica (Argenta ware), impressed marks and date code for 1872, length 10″.

Figure 189. Wedgwood majolica (Argenta ware) oyster plate, *below*, impressed marks and date code for 1878, diameter 9″.

Figure 190. Wedgwood majolica garden pot, *left*, in the "Magnolia" pattern on conforming pedestal, impressed marks and date code for 1877, height 40½". The somber taste in some Victorian interiors could not accommodate the colorful majolica, and dark, contrasting tones of brown, green or plum were favored. Jardinieres of this large scale were intended to hold aspidistras.

Figure 191. Wedgwood majolica dessert plate, *above*, of Limoges form decorated in the center with the [Baron du] *Tremblay* or *Email Ombrant* technique, diameter 8½". The *Email Ombrant* technique, whereby a design molded in intaglio or shallow relief is given perspective through a coating of translucent glaze, was developed in France by Baron du Tremblay in the 1840s and examples were shown at the Great Exhibition. In 1872, Wedgwood purchased more than 2,500 *Tremblay* molds, designs, and glaze recipes, together with his original patent, and began using them prolifically, mostly on dessert services. *Collection of Lloyd J. Bleier*

Figure 192. Wedgwood majolica umbrella stand, *right*, patterned with flora and fruit, impressed marks and date code for 1891, height 23". *Collection of Mr. & Mrs. G. Leberfeld*

Figure 193. Impressed marks of the type found on most Wedgwood majolica, *below*. For an explanation of the code, see page 108.

George Jones

The majolica ware manufactured by George Jones of Stoke-on-Trent is among the most avidly sought by modern collectors and is well respected for its consistently high quality in design and execution.

The manufacturer was unique in Staffordshire as a specialist in the design and manufacture of majolica ware, which accounted for over 70 percent of the company's products in 1875,[36] and thus the term "true majolica" used earlier in this book to describe objects designed exclusively for manufacture as majolica ware can be applied to virtually all of George Jones's products. The manufacturer exhibited widely, including the International Expositions in Paris (1867), London (1871), Vienna (1873), and Sydney (1876), but did not approach the size of Minton's or Wedgwood's and concentrated on production of "useful" wares, many designed for uniquely Victorian occasions (Figures 205 and 207).

George Jones (c. 1824–1893) received his apprenticeship as a potter at Minton's in the early 1850s,[37] where he was exposed to the technical and artistic excellence and progressive ideals of Leon Arnoux and the earliest forms of English majolica production. By 1861, he was sufficiently capable and independent to establish the "Trent Potteries" in Stoke-on-Trent, which continued to operate as George Jones & Sons until the early years of this century. The firm was known as the "Crescent Pottery" until its take-over by the Brains Company in 1951.

George Jones's majolica output displays a remarkable and ambitious variety of forms, with production models ranging from ash trays to impressive trefoil jardiniere centerpieces for conservatories (Figures 198 and 199). Among Jones's more innovative majolica products were a dog trough (Figure 200), a series of four-footed cen-

Figure 194. George Jones majolica dessert plate, *left*, in the "Lily Pad" pattern, circa 1870, diameter 8". George Jones is commonly credited with the introduction of the water lily pad design that was adopted by the numerous English, Continental, and American manufacturers of majolica and is available in reproduction today. *Collection of Dr. & Mrs. Howard Silby*

Figure 195. George Jones majolica teakettle, *above*, in the "Pineapple" pattern, circa 1870, height 8". George Jones excelled in the design and production of useful ware. This is the larger of two versions that were made of the same design; milk jugs, sugar bowls, and cups and saucers in the same pattern were also available. *Collection of Mr. & Mrs. G. Leberfeld*

Figure 196. George Jones majolica Stilton cheese stand and cover, *above*, in the "Apple Blossom" pattern, circa 1875, height 7". George Jones offered a range of seven Stilton cheese stands, including two sizes in this popular pattern. *Collection of J. Garvin Meeking, Inc.*

Figure 197. Design drawings, *right*, for five models from George Jones's seven majolica Stilton cheese stands, circa 1875. George Jones delighted in whimsical and innovative design treatment of ordinary objects. *Trustees of the Wedgwood Museum, Barlaston, Staffordshire, England*

Figure 198. George Jones majolica ashtray, *above*, with handle in the form of an inquisitive fox (design number 3280), circa 1880, length 4″. Ashtrays complemented complete George Jones smoking sets, which included a quatrefoil tray, a spill vase, a covered cigar box, a covered lucifer (match) box, a covered tobacco box, and an ashtray. Three designs were offered featuring dogs, cats, and foxes. *Collection of Dr. & Mrs. Howard Silby*

Figure 199. Design for George Jones's largest and, at £10.10, his most expensive, majolica production model, *right*, circa 1889. This adventurous jardiniere design, intended as a free-standing conservatory centerpiece, was available at a lower cost without the three projecting pots and stands at its base. The lilies, naturalistically modeled in bold relief, are unmistakably George Jones. *Trustees of the Wedgwood Museum, Barlaston, Staffordshire, England*

terpieces with figural stems that were allegorical of continents (Figure 51),[38] menu and place card holders, Stilton cheese stands (Figures 196 and 197), spittoons, including one remarkable example naturalistically formed as a tortoise (Figure 201), and a caviar server.

George Jones drew artistic inspiration from a wide variety of sources, including his son, Horace, who worked as a designer and modeler at the works following his studies at the South Kensington Art School in the mid-1870s. Many of the designs are predictable, in the popular academic taste dictated mainly by Minton's (Figure 204), and include such familiar objects as cake stands, bread trays, game pie dishes (six designs of which were offered), sardine and potted meat boxes (Figure 286), candlesticks, as well as the usual wide variety of table and tea ware and requisites for the conservatory—jardinieres, wall pockets, and hanging pots. The versatility of George Jones's designers is evident in the many whimsical models produced in majolica, which represent an inspired Victorian culture, unaffected at the conception stage by traditional or imposed guidelines upon design. These include the models that evoke a pun, the source of great amusement for Victorians "at home," notably the delightful "Punch" bowl (Figure 205).

Along with whimsy, George Jones's majolica excels in the depiction of naturalistic motifs, especially common British birds, which have perhaps never found more sympathetic treatment in the history of decorative earthenware (Figure 207). Finches, robins, kingfishers, wrens, wagtails, blue tits, and sparrows, as well as swans and doves, adorn a wide variety of useful and decorative wares and were available as optional extras, usually for a cost of a few more pence, on several models, as were butterflies, modeled naturalistically in full relief.[39]

The use of common British flora and fauna was especially suitable for George Jones's rustic style, which is uniquely English in inspiration and evocation (Figure 211) George Jones was not limited to this taste, however, and the design repertoire included elaborate, revivalist ware of Continental taste (Figure 209) and progressive designs showing Japanese derivation. One strikingly distinct model that illustrates Jones's abilities as a "modern" designer is the teapot illustrated in Figure 210, which may have been designed by Horace Jones. The teapot, based in form on a Japanese iron kettle, shows the elegant simplicity associated with the ideals of Charles Eastlake and Dr. Christopher Dresser.

Figure 202. Pair of George Jones majolica fox-and-hound centerpieces, *above*, in typical palette, circa 1875, height 10″. *Collection of Joan Esch; photograph by Gary Samson*

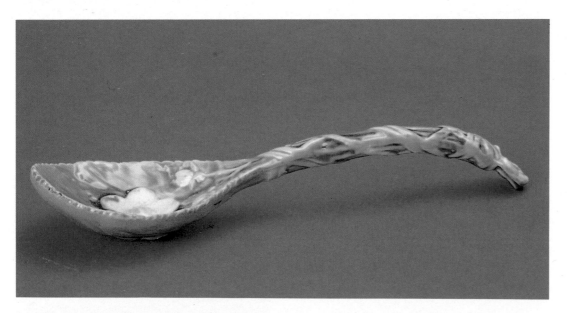

Figure 203. George Jones majolica spoon, *above*, circa 1875, length 7″. Spoons of this type were used to ladle cream or condiments and were usually included with strawberry dishes. *Collection of Joan Esch; photograph by Gary Samson*

Figure 204. Design for a George Jones majolica oyster plate, *above*, circa 1875. George Jones served his apprenticeship at Minton, and many of his products were designed to satisfy the market that the larger company's majolica ware had created. *Trustees of the Wedgwood Museum, Barlaston, Staffordshire, England*

Majolica

Figure 205. George Jones majolica "Punch" bowl, *above*, circa 1870, height 8¼", diameter 11". A fine example of Victorian whimsical design for which majolica ware was well-suited and in which the George Jones Company excelled. Specialized objects of this type were made for Victorians of modest wealth, many of whom lived, customarily, in houses of palatial proportions built to accommodate their large families and staff of servants. Festive family occasions, especially Christmas, for which this bowl was specifically designed, were grand and important events in such households. *Collection of Mr. and Mrs. G. Leberfeld*

Figure 206. Design drawing for the George Jones majolica "Punch" bowl, *left*, circa 1878. The holly motif encircling the bowl suggests this model was designed for use at Christmastime. *Trustees of the Wedgwood Museum, Barlaston, Staffordshire, England*

Figure 207. George Jones majolica strawberry server, *left*, circa 1875 (design number 2217), length 15″. The popularity of strawberry servers can be attributed in part to the proliferation of hothouses in Victorian homes during the 1870s and 1880s, and they are typically found in majolica or silver plate. Few examples were made after about 1890. *Collection of Mr. and Mrs. G. Leberfeld*

Figure 208. Design for a candlestick in silver, *right*, English, circa 1850. The modeling of birds in full relief was popular in English decorative art during the mid-nineteenth century and by no means an invention of George Jones, although he exploited the technique to a highly successful degree as a potter's art (see Figure 207).

Figure 209. George Jones majolica fruit tray, *below*, with central handle modeled as a bacchanal, the dish wells patterned with grapevines and spreading palm fronds, circa 1865, length 13½″. A well-modeled and well-executed example of George Jones majolica in the Minton taste. *Collection of Dr. & Mrs. Howard Silby*

Figure 212. George Jones majolica teapot, *left*, of rooster form, circa 1876, length 11". A fine example of George Jones's "whimsical" production models. *Collection of Mr. and Mrs. G. Leberfeld*

Figure 213. George Jones majolica dessert plate, *below*, patterned with foliage, circa 1875, diameter 8½". *Collection of Dr. & Mrs. Howard Silby*

Figure 210. George Jones majolica teakettle, *opposite above*, (design number 2755) and flower pot, the designs attributed to Horace Jones, circa 1877; height of the taller, 6". The sparsely decorated kettle, which was also available with a "rustic"-style stand, is a unique example of the influence of progressive Japanese taste on George Jones majolica. These two examples are unmarked. *Collection of Mr. and Mrs. G. Leberfeld*

Figure 211. Five designs from the small range of majolica tiles, *opposite*, produced at the Trent potteries of George Jones & Sons, Stoke-on-Trent, circa 1880. George Jones did not compete strongly in the decorative tile market, and examples from this factory, all of which were majolica-glazed, are rare. *Trustees of the Wedgwood Museum, Barlaston, Staffordshire, England*

Following the lead of Minton's and others, George Jones began introducing decorative porcelain and *pâte-sur-pâte*–type ware about 1880, together with a small range of decorative earthenwares sparsely printed with *Japonesques*.[40] These new lines were clearly in response to the declining market for majolica ware, identified by Charles Bachhoffner and others (see page 108), and were not the company's forte. The *pâte-sur-pâte* in particular, only nine designs for which are recorded, was mostly of inferior, industrially produced type,[41] although a few exhibition standard examples, modeled by F. Schenck and others, were produced in the mid-1880s.

George Jones majolica is glazed in a characteristic palette of rich, lustrous colors that were probably developed within the pottery. Familiar colors include "Celadon" green, "Snowdrop" white, "Pompadour," a rosy pink commonly used for the inner surfaces of vessels, blue, green and "Rockingham," a rich, dark brown. A mottled combination of Rockingham and green was frequently applied to the underside of George Jones's ware to give a pleasing "tortoise-shell" effect reminiscent of eighteenth-century creamware (Figure 215). Small areas of the buff-colored body about the size of a fingerprint were left unglazed on the bases of earlier wares and may be painted or scratched with design or batch numbers, which are sometimes the only marks applied to George Jones ware, although the familiar GJ monogram within a circle is often present, impressed and under glaze; this may appear on a raised cartouche. After about 1873, a crescent device bearing the words "& Sons" was added below the monogram. Although George Jones design numbers are consecutive and can thus aid in determining the date a design was first registered, such numbers may not signify the date of manufacture of the objects bearing them, since popular models stayed in production for many years. The numbers for majolica are mostly four digits and range from the low 1,000s (early 1860s)[42] to the high 6,000s (1890s), with numbers between 2,000 and 3,000 indicating a date circa 1875, the peak production period for the company.

W. T. Copeland & Sons

In 1847, William Taylor Copeland, M.P. (1797–1868), a-chieved full control of the prestigious firm established by Josiah Spode in the late eighteenth century and enjoyed widespread success as a manufacturer of decorative porcelain and some earthenwares in the highest early Victorian tradition, including a full range of Parian statuary and decorative wares introduced in 1842.

In 1867, Copeland took his four sons into partnership and traded under the name of W.T. Copeland & Sons. Throughout the principal period of majolica production in the Staffordshire Potteries, the Copeland firm was one of the largest establishments, on a scale comparable to Minton and Wedgwood, but majolica ware represented only a small portion of its output.

Copeland excelled in the development and employment of refined porcelain and earthenware bodies, including a highly praised "Ivory" body that was mostly used for table earthenwares but was also used for most Copeland majolica ware (Figure 97). Very delicate and thinly potted, the body can be mistaken for porcelain, which Copeland also used occasionally for majolica-glazed objects. Copeland was also an important manufacturer of architectural majolica, including glazed tiling that was highly regarded. The Copeland Company, which continues operations in Stoke-on-Trent to the present day, with family involvement, enjoyed royal and international patronage and contributed successfully to all the major international exhibitions of the late nineteenth and early twentieth centuries, including the Philadelphia Centennial in 1876 (Figure 217).

During the majolica period, the Copeland firm employed a wide range of printed and impressed marks, and unmarked examples of this ware are rare.

Figure 216. A Copeland green-glazed vine leaf plate, diameter 8½", impressed COPELAND, circa 1865. *Collection of Dr. & Mrs. Howard Silby*

Joseph Holdcroft

Joseph Holdcroft was a local potter who established the Sutherland Pottery[43] at Daisy Bank in Longton in 1870. The firm continued under his name until 1906, when it became Holdcroft's Ltd., and eventually went out of business in the 1920s. Like George Jones, Joseph Holdcroft began his career as an apprentice with Minton's, in the early 1850s, where he was employed in various capacities related to earthenware manufacture for a total of eighteen years. Holdcroft's long period of employment at Minton coincided with the development of majolica under Leon Arnoux, and this unique exposure helped qualify him to establish his own factory. Little is known of his first independent works, which was probably established in 1868, but the products we are familiar with today were all manufactured at the Sutherland Pottery, where Holdcroft specialized in majolica ware together with other domestic earthenwares, including silver luster and Parian porcelain. The period of Joseph Holdcroft's production saw increased demand for majolica from abroad, and many of his products were tailored for the important markets of South America, Australia, and the United States.[44]

The Sutherland Pottery was slightly smaller in scale than the Trent Potteries of George Jones, and Holdcroft's majolica was designed and manufactured very much after the Jones model.

Holdcroft's typical body for majolica is a simple buff earthenware of brittle type much like that used by Jones. The palette of colors is also very comparable and was probably derived from the

Figure 218. Detail of the printed mark, *above*, on Figure 217, including the name of the New York retailer for which this model was exclusively manufactured. *Collection of Mr. & Mrs. G. Leberfeld*

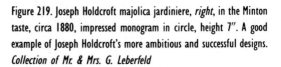
Figure 219. Joseph Holdcroft majolica jardiniere, *right*, in the Minton taste, circa 1880, impressed monogram in circle, height 7". A good example of Joseph Holdcroft's more ambitious and successful designs. *Collection of Mr. & Mrs. G. Leberfeld*

same supplier. Furthermore, Joseph Holdcroft preferred the characteristic style of rustic and natural modeling that George Jones had pioneered, especially in the form of common British bird motifs, and his design repertoire included a number of earlier nineteenth-century models reproduced in majolica glazes. Thus, in many respects, it is justifiable to consider Joseph Holdcroft as a follower of George Jones. This claim is further evidenced by the similarities between their marks, notably those of the small impressed "monogram in circle" type. Some Holdcroft majolica is marked with an impressed "HOLDCROFT," sometimes including an initial J.

Figure 220. Joseph Holdcroft majolica compote, *above*, the support modeled as a gypsy boy, height 8", impressed JH monogram in circle. *Collection of Mr. & Mrs. G. Leberfeld*

Figure 221. Joseph Holdcroft majolica vase of waisted form, *opposite*, circa 1875, height 10¾". *Collection of Dr. & Mrs. Howard Silby*

Figure 222. An English majolica footed bowl, *right*, attributed to Joseph Holdcroft, circa 1875, 13¼". Many of the products of the smaller Staffordshire manufacturers were of high quality in design and execution. This model is in the popular Renaissance Revival taste. *Britannia, Gray's Antique Market, London*

Figure 224. Joseph Holdcroft majolica cheese stand patterned with blackberries, *below*, circa 1875, impressed HOLDCROFT, height 11½". The majolica of Joseph Holdcroft is often very similar to that of the larger and more successful company of George Jones, whose products Holdcroft imitated. *Britannia, Gray's Antique Market, London*

Figure 223. A pair of English majolica figural table salts, *above*, attributed to Joseph Holdcroft, modeled in eighteenth-century taste, circa 1875, height 10½". Eighteenth-century Continental porcelain models provided inspiration for a variety of mid-Victorian ceramics, notably porcelain and Parian ware, and some majolica, including these examples, which are derived from Meissen originals. *Britannia, Gray's Antique Market, London*

Figure 225. Joseph Holdcroft majolica stork vase, circa 1875, impressed JOSEPH HOLDCROFT, height 15″. *Collection of Mr. & Mrs. G. Leberfeld*

S. Fielding & Co.

Majolica ware that bears the Fielding trademark was manufactured at the Railway Pottery in Stoke-on-Trent, established by Simon Fielding (died 1906) in 1870. The company manufactured a wide range of decorative earthenwares including terra-cotta, blackware, brown (Rockingham), and green-glazed articles, and achieved success in majolica production largely due to Abraham Fielding (1854–1932), who served as an apprentice colormaker during the early years of his father's production at the Railway Pottery, and who took control of the financially ailing[45] company in 1878. Abraham Fielding immediately implemented a policy of expansion and, in 1880, the works was enlarged to facilitate production of new types of earthenware, including a range of "majolica Argenta" in the manner of Wedgwood's Argenta ware, with a pale body sparsely decorated with majolica glazes (Figure 239). Fielding offered a wide range of useful and decorative articles including "all the minutiae of the table,"[46] for markets at home and abroad.

Abraham Fielding, who regularly cycled to work on his pennyfarthing bicycle,[47] was a well-respected local figure and became president of the local Ceramics Society in later life. He successfully steered the company into the twentieth century, when Fielding's concentrated on the manufacture of decorative earthenwares and porcelain under the "Crown Devon" trademark. Fielding majolica is not always marked, but marks include an impressed "FIELDING," or printed variations of the name "SF and Co."

Figure 226. A jug, *below left*, in a popular version of the shell-and-seaweed pattern also called shell-and-net, by S. Fielding & Co., circa 1878, unmarked, height 9". *Collection of Mr. & Mrs. G. Leberfeld*

Figure 227. An S. Fielding & Co. majolica pickle dish, *below*, 1882, length 7", impressed FIELDING, with registry mark. *Collection of Mr. & Mrs. G. Leberfeld*

Brown-Westhead, Moore & Co.

In 1858, the Ridgway family's prestigious Shelton Works, established by Job Ridgway in 1802, was taken over by managing partners and became Bates, Brown-Westhead & Co. In 1862, the company traded under the name of its two principal partners, T.C. Brown-Westhead, and William Moore (1822–1866), the highly respected works manager under John Ridgway, who died in 1860. Chiefly under the guidance of William Moore, who died prematurely in mid-term of office as mayor of Hanley, leaving two sons who later continued the business, Brown-Westhead, Moore & Co. pursued a policy of expansion and concentration upon production of decorative glazed earthenwares, some of which evolved from the firm's introduction of sanitary ware (to meet the market demands explained in chapter 1), which they first displayed successfully at the Great Exhibition of 1851. The company continued to use national and international exhibitions as a forum for new products and was awarded the *Grand Prix* (the highest award in its class) at the Paris Exhibition of 1889, by which time they were using the familiar trademark "Cauldon," named for their works at Cauldon Place. The company followed Minton's lead by employing French design talent, notably Antonin Boullemier, who painted at the works in the late 1880s.[48]

Brown-Westhead, Moore & Co. invested heavily in the potential of majolica and other decorative earthenwares abroad. Promotional campaigns targeted foreign markets, especially in the later years of the majolica period, when the principal demand for English majolica was from export trade, and Brown-Westhead, Moore & Co. can be largely credited with generating the popularity that majolica enjoyed in the United States, where the company had an extensive network of

Figure 228. Brown-Westhead, Moore & Co. earthenware vase, *left*, of majolica type, exhibited at Philadelphia in 1876.

Figure 229. Majolica square teapot, *below*, patterned with blackberries attributed to Brown-Westhead, Moore & Co., circa 1885, unmarked, height 7″. A typical example of the later majolica products of Staffordshire manufacturers, this teapot is comparable in style to the American-made ware produced to compete with it. *Britannia, Gray's Antique Market, London*

agents, in the last quarter of the nineteenth century. By 1880, the company had expanded to include a site spread over seven acres, containing eighteen kilns and employing 1,500 workers.[49]

The company's early majolica, featuring "a rich creamy body covered with a thick luscious glaze, bright lustrous ground tints, and paintings in the color of nature"[50] was praised by contemporary critics, but much of the export-type production in the later majolica period was criticized as too conventional.

Despite frequent mention in contemporary journals as majolica manufacturers, it is important to remember that the principal thrust of Brown-Westhead, Moore & Co. was in the direction of sanitary ware and decorative earthenwares of stoneware type. They were particularly adept in the manufacture of pan closets, the contemporary formal term for toilet bowls, which the Victorians delighted in designing and for which the company claimed Royal patronage.[51] One documented example designed by a Mr. Jennings of London required the work of four molders to cast and assemble the sixteen components.[52] An impressive collection of Victorian pan closets, some of which are finished in majolica glazes, is on discreet display at the Gladstone Pottery Museum in Longton.

Figure 230. Group of earthenware by Brown-Westhead, Moore & Co., from the Philadelphia Centennial Exhibition, 1876.

Royal Worcester

Worcester porcelain, made in the city of Worcester, some sixty miles south of the Potteries, has a celebrated and continuous history dating back to 1751. Throughout its history, including during the majolica period, the company concentrated on the manufacture of decorative porcelain, and earthenwares have always represented a small proportion of its output. Some examples of Royal Worcester majolica glazed ware using a pale buff-colored earthenware body are recorded, however, and are of characteristic high quality in design and execution (Figures 231, 232, and 233). Typically, these include familiar and popular Royal Worcester porcelain table ware models, all of which bear the impressed or printed roundel mark that has appeared on all Royal Worcester products since 1862.

Figure 232. Royal Worcester majolica shell-and-dolphin centerpiece, *above*, impressed roundel mark, circa 1875, height 6½". Royal Worcester majolica-glazed earthenware is uncommon. The company concentrated on the design and manufacture of useful and decorative porcelains, and most majolica models, including this example, appear more frequently in porcelain. *Collection of Dr. & Mrs. Howard Silby*

Figure 231. Majolica teapot, *above*, modeled as a fish swallowing another fish, popularly attributed to Royal Worcester, circa 1880, height 6", unmarked. The common attribution of this familiar model is suspect, and it is most likely the product of a Staffordshire manufacturer. *Collection of Mr. & Mrs. G. Leberfeld*

Figure 233. A pair of Royal Worcester majolica wall pockets, *right*, modeled as reed warbler's nests, circa 1875, height 9". Ceramic wall pockets have been popular in English domestic interiors since the middle of the eighteenth century and have been manufactured in porcelain at Worcester since then. They enjoyed a surge in popularity during the period of mid-Victorian fascination with hothouses and conservatories and this pair is a good example of innovative design intended to meet this demand. *Collection of Dr. & Mrs. Howard Silby*

Other English Manufacturers

By the time of the Great Exhibition, the Potteries of North Staffordshire was home to 133 factories, two-thirds of the British pottery industry, employing over 40,000 people.[53] Throughout the last half of the century, dozens of these manufacturers made majolica-glazed earthenwares, exclusive of the principal manufacturers described above. These other factories varied in scale from works of several hundred employees to tiny pot works, typically employing a dozen or so people and two bottle ovens (kilns). Many relied upon their larger and more resourceful colleagues to establish trends and promote markets, which they subsequently followed rather than acting as innovators of taste or technical achievement. The products of these companies appear frequently in the collector's marketplace, and those that bear marks of manufacturers offer enticement for further research into what can often be a murky and poorly documented history. Perhaps the largest of this genre of manufacturers was the company operated by William Brownfield (1812–1873) in Codbridge, where majolica was manufactured from 1860 until 1900, when the works was demolished. From 1871, the art director was Louis Jahn, who had received his training at Minton's, and in the 1880s upwards of 600 people were employed there in the manufacture of all types of decorative earthenware, especially transfer printed ware, and some majolica was made for the United States, Canadian, and Continental markets as well as for the home trade. Marks include an elaborate printed device with the name Brownfield & Son within a ribbon and a simple printed Staffordshire knot encircling the letters WB. Most Brownfield majolica ware is unmarked, however, although registry marks may be present.

Other manufacturers of English majolica whose products can sometimes be identified through marks or contemporary documentation include the Brownhills Pottery Company, which operated between about 1871 and 1896 (Figures 235 and 237); Samuel Lear, who made and decorated majolica at his Hanley Works between 1877 and 1880; Messrs. Banks and Thorley, and Wardle and Co. of Hanley (Figure 238); Shorter and Boulton, and Adams and Bromley of Stoke-on-Trent, who concentrated on majolica for the United States and Australian markets from 1879 until closure in 1905; and Edward Steele of the Cannon Street Works in Hanley (1875–1900), who made a full range of good quality but unmarked majolica ware.

Figure 234. Advertisement for Thomas Forestor, *above*, one of dozens of smaller Victorian manufacturers of majolica and other decorative earthenware located in the Staffordshire potteries. The *pompadour* majolica, as advertised by Forestor, refers to ware of pink ground color that evokes the celebrated *Rose Pompadour* of eighteenth-century Sèvres porcelain, which was first used by Minton and later adopted by most majolica makers. *Reproduced from* The Pottery Gazette, *1882*

Figure 235. English majolica owl jug, *above*, circa 1885, height 12″. This model was made by a smaller Staffordshire manufacturer, possibly William Brownfield, and was popular during the 1880s, when it was made in several sizes, this being the largest. *Britannia, Gray's Antique Market, London*

Most majolica products of the smaller English manufacturers are unmarked, but can be readily identified by consistency in materials and standards of manufacture and decoration. English design registration marks appear on a wide range of ceramics and other categories of design made between 1842 and 1883 (Figures 237 and 243), and their presence can be considered evidence of English origin, although some continental designs were occasionally registered in England. The mark can be impressed or printed, and is of a standard diamond shape that features letters or numerals in each angle, which can be read to indicate the date, month, and year in which the design of the object was officially registered (as a form of copyright protection). A key table for these marks is included here. After 1884, registry marks are typically in the form of printed numbers with the prefix "Rd No." These numbers begin with number 1 in January 1884, and were used consecutively until January 1909, when the numbers reached 550,000.[54]

Most of the smaller English manufacturers began majolica production in the later years of the majolica period, capitalizing on the successes of Minton, and many of their products were designed for foreign markets, including South America and Africa. Such wares can be identified by the frequent use of exotic ornament and motifs, parrots, African animals, tropical foliage, and more (Figure 242).

Figure 236. Majolica jug, *above*, in Wedgwood taste by the Brownhills Pottery Company, printed mark and registry mark for 1878, height 7". *Collection of Mr. & Mrs. G. Leberfeld*

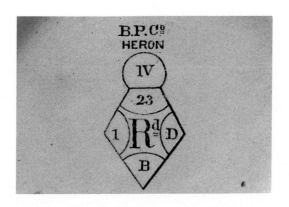

Figure 237. Printed mark of the Brownhills Pottery Company, *left*, including registry mark for the year 1878 (see Figure 243).

Figure 238. English majolica set tea, *above*, in the "Fern and Bamboo" pattern, attributed to Wardle and Company of Hanley, circa 1875, height of teapot 6½". *Collection of Mr. & Mrs. G. Leberfeld*

Figure 239. Majolica moustache cup and saucer, *left*, Staffordshire, circa 1880, indecipherable registry mark, diameter of saucer 7". Moustache cups were popular with gentlemen of the mid-Victorian era. This example is stylistically typical of the majolica Argenta produced by Simon Fielding and others in the 1880s. *Collection of Dr. & Mrs. Howard Silby*

Figure 240. English majolica wine jug, *opposite*, attributed to Brown-Westhead, Moore & Co. circa 1885, height 8½". The coloration quality and design of this object identify it as a product of the later majolica period that was made primarily for export. *Britannia, Gray's Antique Market, London*

Figure 241. Majolica teapot of good quality, Staffordshire, circa 1870, height 7½". The high standards of design and execution of this example suggest a large and accomplished manufacturer. *City Museum and Art Gallery, Stoke-on-Trent*

Figure 242. Staffordshire majolica jug, registry mark for 1880, height 6". This is a typical example of the inexpensive decorative majolica made by smaller Staffordshire manufacturers for foreign (probably tropical) markets toward the end of the majolica period. *Collection of Mr. & Mrs. G. Leberfeld*

English Registry Marks

Design registration marks may appear impressed, printed, or molded onto English majolica ware. All will bear the class number "IV," for ceramics and glass, and letters that can be read to reveal the date the design was registered (for copyright protection), which is not necessarily the date the object was manufactured. The system was in use between 1842 and 1883, an index to the year and month letters is included below:

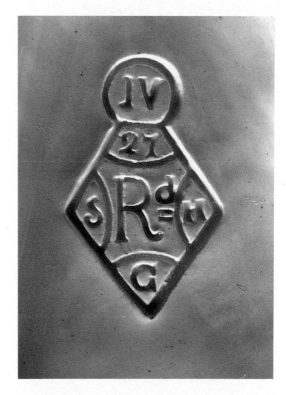

Figure 243. Impressed English registry mark of a type found on ceramics (and some glass) between 1842 and 1883. This mark reveals that the design was registered in 1869. The year and month letters are for February 27.

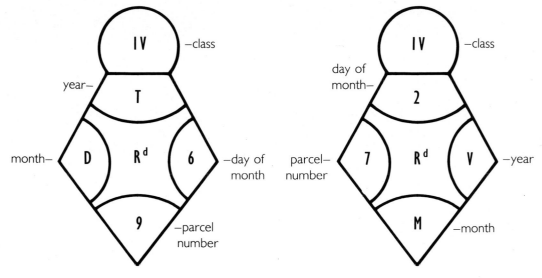

Years

1842–1867
Year letter at top

A = 1845	J = 1854	S = 1849
B = 1858	K = 1857	T = 1867
C = 1844	L = 1856	U = 1848
D = 1852	M = 1859	V = 1850
E = 1855	N = 1864	W = 1865
F = 1847	O = 1862	X = 1842
G = 1863	P = 1851	Y = 1853
H = 1843	Q = 1866	Z = 1860
I = 1846	R = 1861	

1868–1883
Year letter at right

A = 1871	I = 1872	U = 1874
C = 1870	J = 1880	V = 1876
D = 1878	K = 1883	W = 1878 (1–6 March)
E = 1881	L = 1882	X = 1868
F = 1873	P = 1877	Y = 1879
H = 1869	S = 1875	

Months
(both periods)

A = December	E = May	I = July	M = June
B = October	G = February	K = November (and December 1860)	R = August (and September 1–19, 1857)
C or O = January	H = April		
D = September			W = March

Majolica in Continental Europe

Figure 244. French majolica dessert service, *opposite above*, of good quality in the English taste, circa 1875–1880. The design of this dessert service is clearly inspired by English majolica, but the coloration, especially the characteristic mustard ground, and thickly potted body suggest Continental origin. *Collection of Dr. & Mrs. Howard Silby*

The English Taste and Palissy Ware

By the third quarter of the eighteenth century, England was established as the principal manufacturer of decorative earthenwares for the Western world, with production centered in Staffordshire, the heartland, a phenomenon that continues to the present day. Despite the overwhelming superiority—technically, artistically, and commercially—of English majolica, which successfully eliminated American competition, a number of Continental and Scandinavian manufacturers chose to compete in the market. Typically, Continental majolica reflects the contemporary superiority of the English product in that it is either an interpretation of exported English majolica (Wedgwood, which has always enjoyed considerable prestige throughout Europe, was a popular target) or it is of a widely different nature, produced in a deliberate effort to avoid foreign competition.

Continental majolica in the English taste was made mostly in France, Germany, and Austria, with most of the output attributed to the Sarreguemines factory in Lorraine. It is in the second category that the most interesting Continental majolica is to be found. Continental majolica of indigenous design, much of which was manufactured at old, established factories, includes contemporary interpretations of historical ceramic art and techniques developed under circumstances parallel to the attempts by Minton and others in Staffordshire to reproduce Renaissance ware. Prominent among these products in the broad category of majolica are the earthenwares made in France and Portugal during the third quarter of the nineteenth century in the manner of Bernard Palissy, the French ceramic genius. Bernard Palissy (1510–1590) was a true Renaissance man. He pursued an active interest in naturalism and potting and

successfully combined the two in his remarkable ceramic achievements, the earliest of which were produced in a homemade kiln at Saintes in about 1539. Palissy's *pieces rustiques*, which included large dishes applied with naturalistically modeled flora and fauna of contemporary appeal, many featuring small reptiles modeled from actual carcasses, are the best known examples of his contribution to ceramic art and represent the style most commonly copied by his followers ever since. Palissy ware produced in France by Charles Jean Avisseau (1796–1861) at his factory in Tours is the most successful, authentic reproduction of the complex work of Palissy (Figure 249), and its realization was an achievement comparable to the best efforts of Leon Arnoux in his early years at Minton.

Although Palissy-style ceramics are commonly considered within the broad range of ware that can be termed "majolica," it is important to consider the fundamental differences between this ware and majolica ware as defined earlier in this book—or as first created by Leon Arnoux. The ceramics of Bernard Palissy were comparable to Victorian majolica in their outrageous design, profusion of ornament, and vivid use of contrasting color. Unlike Victorian majolica, however, within which the colors are achieved, by definition, from the use of opaque or semiopaque colored glazes, Palissy ceramics and their nineteenth-century imitations were painted in metallic enamel colors beneath (and sometimes over) a transparent glaze in conventional fashion. Furthermore, the Victorian product was designed to be manufactured on an industrial scale, using modern techniques of pressing and slip-casting, while the products of Avisseau and others could be manufactured only by precise and skilled methods of hand-modeling and potting, in the sixteenth-century tradition. Both wares achieve their lustrous finish through a process of reduction firing, although this technique was used to a lesser and much more controlled degree in Victorian majolica.

Like Arnoux's earliest efforts, Palissy ware soon evolved from unique authentic reproductions potted in the French tradition and justifiably revered as *confidences d'artistes* into a commercial mainstream product of contemporary forms in interpreted style. Several followers of Avisseau, including members of his family, produced this later ware in France, but the principal manufacturers were in Caldas da Rainha, in Portugal.

Figure 245. Continental "majolica" cruet stand, *left*, probably French, circa 1910. An attractive and whimsical example of the cheap, mass-produced novelty ware that appealed to contemporary tourists. Though commonly classified as majolica, ware of this type can be more accurately considered enameled earthenware, as the colors are typically achieved by underglaze painting, not by application of colored glazes. *Collection of J. Garvin Mecking, Inc.*

Figure 246. A pair of Continental "majolica" flower vases, *right*, modeled as pelicans, probably German, circa 1895, height 13″. A good example of the inexpensive, figural decorative ware made in Continental Europe between circa 1890 and 1920, much of it for export to the United States. *Collection of J. Garvin Mecking, Inc.*

Majolica

Figure 247. Group of German "majolica" smoking articles, circa 1910, height of taller humidor 7½". Smoking requisites were especially popular ceramic products during the early years of the twentieth century. Most were made in Germany for export, and few are marked with anything more than impressed numbers. Novelty and figural designs, many featuring bedouin-type Arabs, abounded. *Collection of Dr. & Mrs. Howard Silby*

As majolica production in the Staffordshire Potteries dwindled in the later years of the century, some continental manufacturers, including Sarreguemines and numerous German and Austrian factories, began concentrating on inexpensive, novelty-type products in majolica glazes, made chiefly for the export market to the United States and Great Britain (Figure 246). This category of ware, which was produced well into the twentieth century, constitutes a sizable proportion of the Continental majolica available to the collector today (Figure 245). The majority of this ware is of trinket type, however, designed to satisfy the whims of late Victorian and Edwardian tourists, and few examples are of esteemed quality in design or execution (Figure 247).

The tendency for continental manufacturers to produce majolica later into the nineteenth century than their English rivals did result in some ware designed in contemporary progressive taste, under the influence of the Art Nouveau movement in France or its *Jugendstijl* form in Germanic and Northern Europe (Figure 248). Following is a list of the principal continental manufacturers of majolica, including their dates of operation and other information.

Figure 248. Majolica jardiniere on stand in Art Nouveau taste, Austrian, circa 1898, height 52″. *Collection of Mr. and Mrs. I. Chisholm*

Avisseau and the Followers of Bernard Palissy

In 1829, Charles Jean Avisseau (1796–1861) established a small pottery in the traditional French potting town of Tours with the objective of reproducing earthenware authentically in the manner of Bernard Palissy. Presumably, Avisseau was inspired by contemporary taste for Renaissance Revivalism and supportive literature, including Schloecher's *La Vie et Travaux de Palissy*, published by the Revue de Paris in 1834, and André Pottier's *Monuments Français Inedits* (1839). The finest examples of this ware, which was made in limited quantity and is rare on the market today, were made by Charles Jean Avisseau at Tours. From about 1850, Palissy ware was also designed at the Tours factory by his daughter, Caroline, and his son, Edward Avisseau (1831–1911), and later by his grandson of the same name (1844–1910). From 1843, designs were produced by Charles Jean Avisseau's brother-in-law, Joseph Landais (1800–1883), who was succeeded by his own son, Alexandre (1868–1912).[1] Several of Avisseau's products, designed by Landais, were included in the Paris Exhibition of 1855 (some of which were subsequently acquired by Henry Cole for the South Kensington Museum), at which time the Tours factory concentrated on authentic Palissy reproductions.

The exposure generated by international exhibitions and museum displays in London and Paris[2] greatly increased public appreciation and, subsequently, demand for Palissy ware. This movement was centered in France, where the romantic appeal of the "artist potter" permeated most of the nineteenth century and had little impact in England.

Following the death of Charles Jean Avisseau, a variety of earthenwares with more modern application were conceived and manufactured, together with a diversity of Renaissance ceramic reproductions, including a version of Henri II ware, which were highly praised at the Paris Exposition of 1867. Other manufacturers of Palissy-style ware at Tours included Leon Brard (1830–1902) and Auguste Chauvigne (1829–1904), both pupils of Charles Jean Avisseau. Manufacturers in Paris included Thomas Sergent, Victor Barbizet (Figure 251), who produced good-quality wares from 1850, and Georges Pull (1810–1889), a former soldier and naturalist who made clever imitations of Palissy ware from about 1856.

Most French potters of this period, including the ones mentioned above, marked their wares with a painted or incised monogram, although many examples are unmarked.

Figure 249. Earthenware platter attributed to C. J. Avisseau in the manner of Bernard Palissy, circa 1855. *Collection of J. Garvin Mecking, Inc.*

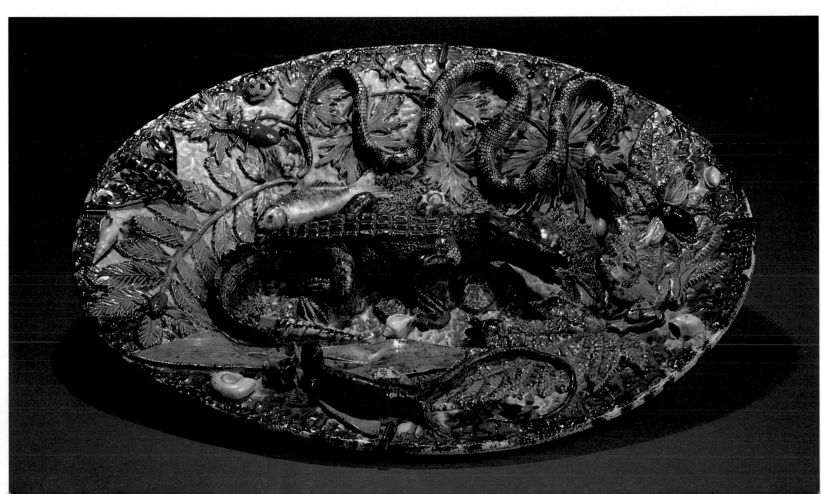

Figure 250. French Palissy style glazed earthenware oyster plate, Tours, circa 1880. The *pièces rustiques* of Bernard Palissy and his followers inspired a variety of nineteenth-century French ceramics, including this successful design which combines the Palissy taste with a modern, commercial form.

Figure 251. Oval platter in Palissy style by Barbizet and Son of Paris, included in the Philadelphia Centennial Exhibition of 1876.

Sarreguemines, Dijoin, and Limoges, Lorraine

A large works was established in this clay-rich part of France by Paul Utzschneider in 1770 and was run by members of the Utzschneider family until the early twentieth century. Until the mid-nineteenth century, the principal product was *faience*, French for tin-glazed earthenware, but a policy of expansion in the 1860s increased the range of output to a variety of decorated earthenwares, including majolica. In 1870, the production of majolica in the English style was increased as the company ordered several Arnoux kilns from Minton to be installed in a new works at Dijoin.[3] The new factory was built to maintain French status for the workers and to ensure their safety following the annexation of parts of the Lorraine region as a consequence of Bismarck's triumph in the Franco-Prussian war. By this time, the pottery was the largest of its type in France, with a work force of over 2,000 employees[4] and products that were surpassed in quality only by Minton. Sarreguemines majolica was manufactured into the early twentieth century and is of uniformly good quality. Products included decorative and useful wares, especially dessert services and well-modeled figural and novelty ware, architectural majolica and tiles, some designed by the English artist Kate Greenaway (1846–1901). A thickly potted, dense body was widely used, which gives Sarreguemines majolica its heavy durable quality. English majolica provided inspiration for many designs, although some products display a uniquely French taste, including those made in the Art Nouveau or *Jugenstijl* styles around 1900. Most are clearly marked, typically with the word "SARREGUEMINES" impressed or with an impressed or printed monogram of the letters "U" and "C" (for Utzschneider et Compagnie), within an octagon (Figure 256).

Figure 252. Two Sarreguemines majolica dessert plates, *above*, from a service of individual fruit pattern, circa 1890. Though much Sarreguemines majolica was designed in English taste, some examples exhibit a uniquely Gallic flavor, including these plates, which have a distinctively French Provincial appeal. Plates of this design have been reproduced in Portugal in recent years. *Collection of Dr. & Mrs. Howard Silby*

Figure 253. French majolica smoking companion, *left*, in the form of a river barge, "L'Hirondelle," attributed to Sarreguemines, circa 1890, length 12½". A clever and appealing design for the novelty market. The foredeck is pierced to hold cigars, the cabin roof lifts off to reveal a compartment for vestas (matches), which can be stuck on the ridged outline of the base. *Collection of J. Garvin Mecking, Inc.*

Figure 254. Sarreguemines majolica cigarette jar in the form of an organ grinder's monkey, circa 1900, height 9¼". A well-modeled and successful example of the novelty ware produced in large quantities at French and German factories from about 1890. *Collection of Mr. & Mrs. G. Leberfeld*

Other French Manufacturers

Other French manufacturers of majolica include Hautin Boulanger et Cie, of Choisy-le-Roi, who produced progessively designed ware in *Japonesque* taste and some majolica, including leaf plates and a version of the shell-and-seaweed motif, during the last quarter of the nineteenth century. A variety of printed marks were used, most incorporating an elaborate printed "HB" monogram.

The firm of Keller et Guerin also made a small quantity of ware that can be classed as majolica in kilns of Arnoux design supplied by Minton's[5] to the historic Luneville works (founded 1731). Products are usually impressed or printed "LUNEVILLE," sometimes with the initials "KG."

A distinctive type of French majolica, one including architectural ware designed and glazed in the Persian taste, was produced at the Boulogne-sur-Seine works of Eugene Victor Collinot (died 1882) between 1862 and about 1902. Collinot was the author of numerous books on decorative arts, including *Ornaments de la Perse*, published in 1859, which inspired decorative and architectural majolica in Persian style. Collinot's work was exhibited at the Paris Exposition of 1867, where it was highly praised by Henry Cole, who acquired several pieces for the South Kensington Museum. Some impressive examples of French majolica were made late in the nineteenth century at the works of Clement Massier (1845–1917) at Golfe Juan, near Cannes. Most examples were highly decorative and large-scale, including jardinieres, and can be attributed to Delphin or Jerome Massier. Clement, the third and better known of the brothers, concentrated on art pottery glazed in the reduction technique. Massier's ceramics were sold through a Paris outlet on the Rue de Rivoli and bear impressed marks that sometimes identify individual family members.

Figure 255. Sarreguemines majolica dessert plate, *above*, of Renaissance revival design, circa 1875, diameter 5¾", impressed monogram mark. *Collection of Dr. & Mrs. Howard Silby*

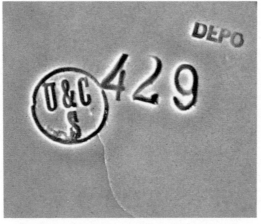

Figure 256. Impressed monogram mark of Messrs. Utzschneider and Co., Sarreguemines, *left*. The impressed DEPO is a shortened form of *Deposé* (confirming a French registered design); the numerals probably refer to a design index. *Collection of Dr. & Mrs. Howard Silby*

Figure 257. Two French majolica hors d'oeuvres dishes, *above*, of provincial taste, for serving lemon slices and olives, circa 1885, diameters 7". *Collection of J. Garvin Mecking, Inc.*

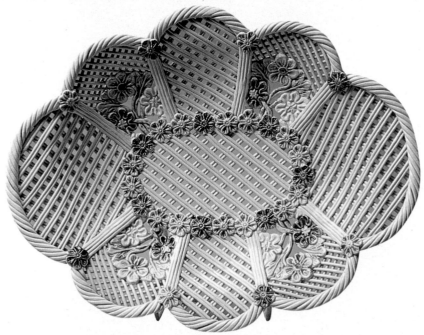

Figure 258. French majolica openwork basket, *left*, circa 1890, length 10". *Collection of Mr. & Mrs. G. Leberfeld*

Figure 259. French majolica and enameled earthenware jardiniere on stand, *left*, by Delphin Massier, circa 1900, height 60″. Flamingos are indigenous to the Languedoc region where Massier worked and were among the most popular exotic images in early twentieth-century French decorative arts. The concept of potting life-scale majolica animal forms was introduced by Minton in the 1860s and rarely practiced elsewhere owing to practical potting and firing difficulties. *Collection of Mr. and Mrs. I. Chisholm*

Figure 260. French majolica and enameled earthenware jardiniere on stand, *right*, by Delphin Massier, circa 1900, height 60″. A good example of French majolica using images drawn from English sources, notably the "Minton peacock," conceived in the flamboyant style, which was popularized at the Paris *Exposition Universelle* of 1900. *Collection of Mr. and Mrs. I. Chisholm*

Figure 261. Continental manufacturers of majolica attracted international trade at the Paris Exposition of 1867, *below*.

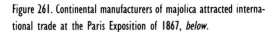

German and Scandinavian Manufacturers

Principal among the German makers of majolica was the firm of Villeroy and Boch. In 1836, the company established in 1748 by François Boch merged with the Villeroy family works, becoming the largest manufacturer of its type in Europe. With production centered at Mettlach in the Rhineland, between circa 1860 and 1900, a large quantity of majolica ware was produced, much of it for export to the United States. Typical products include richly glazed leaf plates and other useful ware, some of English majolica inspiration, which is often distinguishable by the use of semitranslucent, flowing glazes. Architectural majolica was also made, along with a wide range of sanitary ware.

The popular majolica body was of stoneware type, as used on the famous beer steins that the company still manufactures, which gives the majolica a resonant quality. During the early years of the twentieth century, a variety of souvenir ware in majolica glazes was also produced. All products are marked, usually with an impressed or printed roundel including the letters "VBM" (for Villeroy and Boch, Mettlach).

The other German manufacturer of note was Georg Schneider, who produced useful majolica in English style and souvenir ware at the Zell Pottery in Baden (established 1820) from about 1890 to 1920. Most common are dessert plates, including a popular model with rabbit design, some examples of which are marked with a printed cup motif containing the monogram GZS.

Among the small quantity of majolica ware of Scandinavian origin, most can be attributed to the Arabia Pottery, founded in 1874 outside Helsinki, Finland, as a subsidiary of the prestigious Rörstrand Pottery of Sweden. Arabia's principal decorative product was art pottery, the best examples of

which were made during the 1890s using a stoneware body; some were decorated in opaque high glazes that were also used for majolica ware, much of which was designed in *Jugendstijl* taste. Typical examples are functional and large-scale, including jardinieres and plant stands, marked with the word "ARABIA" impressed.

Figure 262. Majolica dessert plate with lily-of-the-valley pattern by Villeroy and Boch, impressed marks, circa 1880, diameter 7¼". *Collection of Dr. and Mrs. Howard Silby*

Figure 263. Impressed monogram mark of Villeroy and Boch, Mettlach, circa 1885. The S stands for Saar, the region where the pottery is situated; the numerals refer to a design index. *Collection of Dr. & Mrs. Howard Silby*

Majolica in Portugal

A large proportion of Victorian Palissy ware was made in Portugal during the last half of the nineteenth century, much of it at the works established in 1853 by Manuel Cyprianio Gomez Mafra at Caldas da Rainha, a traditional potting town where reproduction majolica and Palissy ware is still manufactured (see chapter 7). Credit for the introduction of ware inspired by Bernard Palissy can be given to Manuel Mafra's son, Eduardo, under whose direction the ware was produced until 1897 (Figures 264 and 265), when the factory was taken over by another family member, Cyprianio Gomez Mafra. The products of Mafra are sometimes marked with an impressed device, including the name of the maker and the place of origin.

Another manufacturer of distinctive Palissy-inspired wares at Caldas da Rainha was José A. Cunha, who produced leaf-molded "useful" wares

Figure 264. Portuguese Palissy style oval platter, probably Mafra and Sons, Caldas, circa 1890, length 17". Portuguese imitations of Pallisy's *pièces rustiques* are heavier and less well-modeled than French examples. Many platters feature a ground of simulated "moss," like that used on this example to support the applied figure of a pike. *Phillips, New York*

of bizarre design, some inspired by eighteenth-century tin-glazed earthenwares, around 1900. Examples may bear an impressed mark. In 1883, a large factory was established at Caldas da Rainha by Rafael Bordalo Pinheiro (1845–1905), who designed and made a wide range of majolica-glazed ceramics, including tiles and Palissy ware, examples of which were shown at the Paris Exposition of 1889. The factory continues in production (see chapter 7). The other significant Portuguese ma-

jolica manufacturer was the Manufacture Royale de Rato, in Lisbon, who exhibited a variety of Palissy ware at the Paris Exposition of 1867. All Portuguese Palissy ware, of which Mafra's products are the best quality, is of lesser standard in design and execution than the work of French Palissy imitators from Tours and Paris. The ware tends to be heavy, smaller in scale, and lacking the biological exactitude in modeling in which Palissy and most French followers excelled.

Figure 265. Portuguese Palissy style tea service by Jose A. Cunha, Caldas da Rainha, circa 1890. Ware of this type, combining the bizarre naturalism of sixteenth-century potters with nineteenth-century forms, was made at other works in Caldas da Rainha, and versions are still produced in Portugal today. *Collection of J. Garvin Mecking, Inc.*

Figure 266. Impressed mark of Jose A. Cunha on the teapot illustrated in Figure 265. *Collection of J. Garvin Mecking, Inc.*

6

Majolica in America

Figure 267. The New York Crystal Palace Exhibition, 1853.

A

**Fledgling
American
Industry**

During the third quarter of the nineteenth century, when the industry of majolica production was born and grew to maturity in England, the United States claimed only a fledgling industry in ornamental ceramics, which failed consistently in the face of foreign competition. Indeed, the overwhelming superiority of imported ware, most of it from Staffordshire, encouraged the few rival domestic manufacturers to do little more than imitate foreign designs, sometimes going so far as to add pseudo-English marks to their own products.

This state of affairs was tackled at a governmental level in 1861, when Congress imposed a duty of up to 45 percent on most classes of imported ceramics.[1] One effect of this legislation was to encourage English manufacturers, some of whom were concentrating on the export market, to investigate the potential of manufacturing in the United States. Ironically, in a pattern that mirrored the migration of Staffordshire talent and capital to America a century earlier, the results of which were mostly failures, surnames well known in the Staffordshire Potteries began appearing again in the annals of American ceramic history as the industry embarked upon an era of expansion that would continue into the twentieth century.

In January of 1875, the first National Association of Potters was formed in Philadelphia at a meeting of representatives from seventy factories around the country. Most of them were from the established manufacturing centers in the area of East Liverpool, Ohio, where small potteries had first appeared in the 1820s, and Trenton, New Jersey, which was known as the "Staffordshire of America" by the 1870s,[2] when about twenty factories worked fifty-seven

Figure 268. An Etruscan majolica begonia leaf dish, "a favorite with everyone," by Griffen, Smith & Hill, Phoenixville, Pennsylvania, circa 1885, length 9¼". A distinctive and successful example of American-designed majolica, featuring a palette of colors unique to the Phoenixville factory. *Collection of Dr. & Mrs. Howard Silby*

kilns there.[3] By 1893, the Trenton area was home to thirty-seven factories producing about $5 million worth per annum.[4] The potters resolved not to "copy all or nearly all of our patterns from foreign manufacturers," and claimed "sufficient talent in this country to originate new designs, more elegant and more suitable to the needs of the American people."[5] Barely in evidence at the time, American majolica was one product designed specifically to meet such needs. These were accurately defined by one retrospective analyst:

> Up until the advent of American majolica, the household needs in pottery and china had to be imported from England, thus it is not strange that the ware took on a utilitarian form to meet the needs of the American housewife. Teapots, bowls, plates, mustache cups, and butter dishes were more popular than vases with dolphins supporting sea shells and other fancy-shaped majolica . . . the American housewife preferred the simple designs taken from nature and the familiar begonia leaf transformed into a pickle dish was the favorite with everyone[6] (Figure 268).

The potters' enthusiasm and calls for radically new policies and ideas were testimony of the industry's inability to penetrate domestic markets, despite more than a decade of government protectionism. Their meeting in January 1875 was a prelude to the Philadelphia Centennial Exhibition that was planned for the following year, and it was this singular event that provided the impetus the American ceramics industry needed to overcome its stagnation.

The Philadelphia Centennial Exhibition of 1876 was an event of unprecedented proportions in the United States (Figure 269). American and foreign artistic, industrial, and academic achievements were showcased on the huge site, which featured over 180 buildings (very little evidence of which remains)[7] and welcomed over 10 million visitors between the opening day on May 10 and closing in December.[8] On one day alone, September 28, "Pennsylvania Day," more than 270,000 people attended. The Philadelphia Centennial was designed after the standards set by the Great Exhibition in London and its effect upon American industry was as dramatic as that on the English a quarter-century earlier. The impact was felt especially in the field of ceramics, where foreign manufacturers proved to be far advanced technically, artistically, and commercially.

155

Figure 269. View of the main building at the Philadelphia Centennial Exhibition of 1876, after a design by architects Vaux and Radford. The largest of five principal buildings for the exhibition, with a ground plan covering twenty-one acres. The entire site featured 189 separate buildings and pavilions displaying all types of art and industrial design. One which proved especially popular. featured all aspects of modern burial caskets. *Reprinted from* Masterpieces of the Centennial Exhibition, *Vol. III, p.LXXXIX*

The dominance of imported ceramics was evident in displays from leading English potters, including Minton (Figure 270), Maw & Company, Wedgwood, and Brown-Westhead, Moore & Company, all of which showed majolica ware, and a number of continental manufacturers. Competition was not limited to Europe, however. The "Pavilion of the Empire of Japan" was packed with decorative products from a newly commercial country, combining the tradition of centuries of craftsmanship with unbounded enthusiasm for foreign trade. The pavilion proved to be among the most popular of the exhibition and drew overwhelmingly favorable criticism, especially toward the ceramics displayed:

> The exhibition of porcelain and pottery from Japan is far beyond that of any other nation in importance, not only in the extent of its collection and its varied character, but in its general high standard of excellence and in the great superiority of its individual specimens.[9]

The American potters took full advantage of the educational and commercial opportunities presented by the Centennial Exhibition. As Edwin Atlee Barber, the great American ceramic historian of the nineteenth century, observed in 1892, a year before he published his highly comprehensive *Pottery and Porcelain in the United States*:

> The existence of a true ceramic art in this country may be said to have commenced with the fair of 1876, because greater progress has been made within the fifteen years which have elapsed since that important event than during the two centuries which preceded it.[10]

One form of evidence of this "greater progress" was the development of American art pottery, a phenomenon largely due to Japanese influence, which ultimately gave the ceramics industry a new respectability. Progress was also made in experimental production and marketing of new products, some highly innovative and some based on tried-and-tested foreign techniques. American ma-

jolica is an example of the latter trend, and the industry of its production can be considered co-incidental with the period of expansion in the American ceramics industry that began in 1876 and lasted, approximately, until World War I.

Among 592 exhibitors of ceramics at the Centennial, 199 were American, but only about thirty of these included "ornamental and useful wares" in their displays. Most of the exhibitors made industrial ceramics, drain pipes, or roofing tiles, and only two, James Carr of the New York City Pottery and J.E. Jeffords of Philadelphia, showed products that could be considered "American majolica." Although few American manufacturers made opaque glazed ware by 1876, many were technically equipped to do so. The list of potential makers of American majolica included all producers of "granite-ware," a form of inexpensive, general purpose, highly durable ironstone, and "American cream-colored ware," a coarse, low-fired, porus buff earthenware suitable for inexpensive crockery and thrown goods. The successful production of decorative, durable earthenwares in polychromatic, opaque glazes of a standard comparable to Staffordshire products (even in their crudest form), could not be achieved, however, by simply glazing white granite ware or cream-colored earthenware, as was commonly attempted. The success of majolica by Minton's and their followers can be largely attributed to the remarkable abilities in glaze formulation and kiln technology of Leon Arnoux, and that expertise could not be approached by the American potters. They also lacked the purpose-built glost ovens, considered fundamental to the European industry, and did not enjoy access to the economies of scale and support industries, including color-makers, available among Staffordshire Potteries.

Technically, therefore, most American majolica is wholly distinct from the English product and can often be classed as granite or cream-colored ware decorated with colored glazes, which are often translucent (Figure 271). In the immediate post–Centennial period, the main area of American ceramics industry expansion was in the production of granite and cream-colored earthenware. This was made, however, from inexpensive American clays, and in 1881, the industry claimed over 800 potteries, satisfying 50 percent of domestic demand for such wares.[11] The most successful practitioner of the American majolica technique and, arguably, the only significant manufacturer of majolica in the United States was the Pennsylvania company of Griffen Smith & Hill, owners of the "Etruscan majolica" trademark (Figure 272). Its success was due to a well-designed, inexpensive product combined with demand from a rapidly expanding population of American consumers who were beginning to enjoy the affluence and prosperity of a postfrontier United States. It was in this unique climate of entrepreneurial opportunity that vast fortunes and industrial empires were built, but even this market could not sustain products that failed to anticipate and meet standards and demands. As American consumers became increasingly urban and sophisticated, their taste for the crude, colorful American majolica dwindled, and the product that had encouraged expansion in

Figure 270. An impressive Minton majolica fountain shown at the Philadelphia Centennial Exhibition of 1876, where foreign ceramics manufacturers proved to be far more advanced technically, artistically and commercially, than American competitors.

Figure 271. An American majolica pitcher of enameled white granite ware type, molded in relief with an image of "Jumbo," the famous elephant, circa 1882, height 7½". In 1882, the celebrated "Jumbo," an African elephant of gigantic proportions, was sold by the London Zoo to P. T. Barnum, the American showman, amid public uproar in Great Britain. Jumbo toured North America with Barnum's circus, drawing large crowds for three years until he was tragically killed while touring in Ontario, Canada, in 1885. *Collection of J. Garvin Mecking, Inc.*

the industry for over two decades was relegated to fairground prize status. By the mid-1890s, the stigma from which the industry had suffered in the 1860s returned; by 1897, the Sears, Roebuck catalogue, which was crammed with American-made products of every conceivable description but offered only European ceramics, reminded its customers that "American-made crockery is well known to be inferior to the English and French manufacturer."

Most production of majolica in America had ceased by the onset of World War I. A full list of American majolica manufacturers is included here.

Griffen, Smith & Hill: The Phoenixville Pottery

The first evidence of a pottery in Phoenixville, Pennsylvania, was the construction of brick kilns by the Phoenixville Pottery, Kaolin and Firebrick Company on the corner of Starr and Church streets in 1867. The company's principal business was the manufacture of refractory firebricks, made from local clays for use in the surrounding iron industry. By the early 1870s, the company also produced yellow and Rockingham ware, Parian ware made from molds acquired from the American Porcelain Manufacturing Company of Gloucester, New Jersey, and architectural terra cotta.

Renamed Griffen, Smith & Hill in 1879, the pottery was operated by two members of a local ironmaking family, Henry Griffen (1857–1907) and George S. Griffen (1854–1893); they were joined by David Smith (1839–1895), an Englishman who had begun his career in the Potteries, and William Hill. Production of ornamental majolica probably began in 1879,[12] and was immediately successful. In 1880, two new kilns were built at the works to help meet the large orders for majolica ware that the company attracted, including one from the Atlantic & Pacific Tea Company for several thousand small majolica items, mostly milk jugs, that were used as promotional premiums to help the sale of the company's baking powder.[13]

For the next ten years, the Phoenixville Pottery dominated production of ornamental majolica in North America. By 1881, the company had agents in New York City and Baltimore and publicized their products to consumers,[14] who were made increasingly accessible by the railroad building boom, through comprehensive printed catalogs, some devoted exclusively to their "Etruscan majolica" line. The company also relied on national

Figure 272. Three Etruscan majolica butter pats, *above*, by Griffen, Smith & Hill, circa 1883, diameter 3"; the underside of the example in the middle is shown to display the impressed monogram mark. These humble objects, which were extremely inexpensive when new, are among the most successful—and collectible —examples of American majolica ever made. *Collection of Dr. & Mrs. Howard Silby*

Figure 273. Two Etruscan majolica pickle dishes, impressed full roundel marks, diameter 5½". *Collection of Dr. & Mrs. Howard Silby*

Figure 274. A selection of Etruscan majolica in the "Shell and Seaweed" pattern by Griffen, Smith & Hill, circa 1885, height of humidor 6½". *Collection of Dr. & Mrs. Howard Silby*

Figure 275. Wedgwood pearlware nautilus shell sauceboat and stand, circa 1815, length of stand 10". Etruscan majolica "Shell and Seaweed" ware was undoubtedly inspired by Wedgwood designs of the early nineteenth century.

and international exhibitions that flourished in the United States in the wake of the Centennial Exhibition, notably at New Orleans in 1884. By 1885, the works were expanded, and 400 people may have been employed there.[15]

William Hill left the company in the early 1880s, and David Smith, who was largely responsible for the company's success through his commercial and artistic contributions, left in 1889. The works continued in production until 1903 under various names, including The Chester Pottery Company (1894–1899), The Penn China Company (1899–1902), and The Tuxedo Pottery Company (1902–1903), despite a disastrous fire in 1890.[16] It is unlikely that any new majolica was designed after 1890 or that much was even manufactured after this time, when the popularity of the ware declined significantly.

Throughout the peak period of production, "Etruscan majolica" was made in the rudimentary conditions that characterized most North American potteries. It is probable that both the biscuit

Figure 276. Etruscan "Albino majolica" sideplate, *above left*, in the "Coral" pattern, impressed full roundel mark, circa 1883, diameter 8¼". The taste favoring paler colors that inspired Wedgwood's Argenta ware was interpreted in later American majolica, notably at the Etruscan works. *Collection of Dr. & Mrs. Howard Silby*

Figure 277. Etruscan "Albino majolica" sideplate, *above*, in the "Coral" pattern, with shaded pink coral rim, impressed full roundel mark, circa 1883, diameter 8¼". Another example of the "Coral" plate, with even sparser decoration. The technique of applying limited coloration to aquatic designs was learned from Wedgwood, which used it on pearlware in the late eighteenth century. *Collection of Dr. & Mrs. Howard Silby*

Figure 278. Etruscan "Albino majolica" sideplate, *left*, in the "Coral" pattern with gilt rim, circa 1885, diameter 8¼". As the taste for excessive color diminished, some examples of Etruscan majolica were sold entirely "in the white." Such ware is known to collectors today as "Albino majolica," although the term can be considered an oxymoron. *Collection of Dr. & Mrs. Howard Silby*

(initial) and glost (glaze) firings were done in bottle ovens[17] more suited to the production of terra cotta and white granite ware than to ornamental majolica, and certainly the sophisticated techniques and materials employed by Minton and other manufacturers in the Potteries were not present.

The origin of the trade name "Etruscan" is unclear. It may have been chosen as a prestigious term referring to the advanced Etruscan pottery in the Hellenic taste made in the last seven centuries B.C., or, more likely, it was chosen owing to the contemporary popularity of the Etruscan style in revivalist decorative arts. The Etruscan majolica range included a wide variety of useful wares, with many objects and design motifs found exclusively in American majolica, together with a small amount of purely ornamental ware (Figures 280–287).

The body is thickly potted from gray clays and is relatively low-fired, giving it a lightweight, brittle nature and buff color. Most Etruscan majolica is decorated with a muted palette of glazes that often flow into each other in a characteristically American manner. This soft coloration is especially successful when applied to designs of attractive form patterned with elaborate low relief, as well as naturalistic patterns, notably the popular "Shell and Seaweed" line (Figures 272, 273, and 274). Some Etruscan majolica ware was left virtually undecorated or given only a border color in the taste made popular by Wedgwood's Argenta ware. Such ware is commonly referred to today as "Albino majolica" (Figures 276–279).

During the mid-1880s, demands for new majolica designs were high, and it is probable that the Phoenixville art department included Englishmen in exile from the Staffordshire Potteries. One such individual, a Mr. Bourne, is documented as a designer at the Phoenixville Pottery,[18] although little else is known of him. It is likely that David Smith also contributed designs; however, no specific designer records from Phoenixville are known to exist.

Most Etruscan majolica is marked with either a version of the familiar impressed roundel, including a monogram of the initials GSH, or an impressed design number, which may have a letter prefix (Figure 282), or both. The underside of most Etruscan majolica, especially the utilitarian tableware, is typically treated with sparse, colored glazes, applied by sponge in a loose interpretation of the marblizing effect favored by George Jones and other Staffordshire manufacturers (Figure 288).

Figure 279. Etruscan "Albino majolica" maple syrup jug with "Coral" pattern and hinged pewter cover, impressed full roundel mark, circa 1885, height 6½". Ware of this type was a response to the same markets for which Wedgwood produced Argenta ware (see Figures 187–189). *Collection of Dr. & Mrs. Howard Silby*

Figure 285. Etruscan majolica sardine box, cover and stand, impressed full roundel, circa 1875, length of stand 8¾". Inspired by the popular products of George Jones (see Figure 286), this model was later produced with an intrinsic stand. *Collection of Dr. & Mrs. Howard Silby*

Figure 287. Etruscan majolica vase, impressed monogram mark, circa 1879, height 8½". The mottled, muted coloration on the exterior of this vase and the pink interior are highly characteristic of the Etruscan factory palette. *Collection of Dr. & Mrs. Howard Silby*

Figure 288. Underside of an Etruscan majolica dish showing the impressed full roundel mark and characteristic mottled glaze covering, achieved by applying two colors of glaze to the biscuit body with a sponge. *Collection of Dr. & Mrs. Howard Silby*

Figure 286. George Jones majolica sardine box with separate underplate, impressed monogram, circa 1870, length 8½". George Jones's sardine boxes were intended to hold small fish or fish paste, a widely consumed Victorian delicacy, and were among many English majolica designs copied by American manufacturers (Figure 285). *Britannia, Gray's Antique Market, London*

The Bennett Pottery

In 1846, a pottery was established on Canton Avenue in Baltimore, Maryland, by Edwin Bennett, an Englishman who had operated a small works with his brothers for at least five years, first at East Liverpool, Ohio, and then at Birmingham (now a part of Pittsburgh), Pennsylvania. Bennett's factory produced yellow- and "Rockingham"-glazed ware under the name E. & W. Bennett until 1856, when the initial W, for Bennett's brother, William, was dropped. Majolica was probably not made at the works until the late 1870s, by which time Bennett also owned and operated the Chesapeake Pottery of Donald Francis Haynes. Although the Haynes family regained ownership in the mid-1890s, Bennett's Pottery was the largest in the Baltimore area and continued in operation until about 1937.[19] Many examples bear printed marks.

Figure 289. Bennett's Pottery white granite ware maple syrup jug with enameled ornament, printer marks, circa 1880, height 8". Many of the American decorative earthenwares that are broadly termed majolica today were not produced with the use of majolica glazes. *Collection of Dr. & Mrs. Howard Silby*

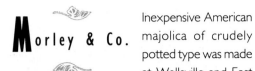orley & Co.

Inexpensive American majolica of crudely potted type was made at Wellsville and East Liverpool, Ohio, by Morley & Co. between circa 1879 and 1885. Examples may bear a printed mark including the word "MAJOLLICA," spelled with two L's (Figures 296 and 297). Majolica of similar type was also made by the neighboring East Liverpool Pottery Company, and examples may be marked with the trademark "TENUOUS MAJOLICA" or the initials "E.L.P. CO."

Figure 295. An American majolica oyster plate, *above left*, attributed to Morley & Co., Wellsville, Ohio, circa 1880, diameter 10". Most majolica oyster plates were of English manufacture, although they were especially popular in the United States. Because American majolica was typically too crude a ware, porcelain manufacturers, such as the Union Porcelain Works of New York, had more commercial success with oyster plates. *Collection of Dr. & Mrs. Howard Silby*

Figure 296. Majolica "napkin plate," *above*, by Morley & Co., Wellsville, circa 1883, printed mark, including the trade name "MAJOLLICA," diameter 8¾". Intended to serve cakes, whereupon a molded napkin replaced the cloth example, "napkin plates," were a popular and whimsical addition to American tables in the 1880s. *Collection of Dr. & Mrs. Howard Silby*

Figure 297. Printed mark of Morley & Co., *above*, circa 1885.

Figure 298. An American majolica cuspidor, *left*, possibly made at the East Liverpool Pottery Company, East Liverpool, Ohio, circa 1885, height 8¼". Decorative spittoons of this type were commonly used in private homes in the late nineteenth century. Those found in public bars, hotel lobbies, and the like, were typically made of brass. *Collection of Dr. & Mrs. Howard Silby*

The New Milford Majolica and Wannopee Pottery Companies

A pottery was established at New Milford, Connecticut, in 1887 for the exclusive manufacture of American majolica of inexpensive type. The company never enjoyed financial success and was liquidated in 1892 when the stock was sold at auction in barrel lots, most of which fetched five cents each.[21] Renamed the Wannopee Pottery Company in the same year, the works specialized in the production of cabbage leaf ware (Figure 300) in eighteenth-century taste, until at least 1904, together with a range of conventional majolica and Rockingham glaze ware including pitchers, candlesticks (Figure 299), umbrella stands, cuspidors, clock cases, jardinieres, and tableware made from the New Milford Majolica Company's molds. Marks of the Wannopee Pottery include an initial W within a sun-in-splendor, and an impressed or painted "WANNOPEE."

Figure 299. Wannopee Pottery Company Rockingham ware candlestick, *left*, in the form of a fire trumpet, impressed mark, circa 1895, height 12¼". *Collection of Dr. & Mrs. Howard Silby*

Figure 300. Wannopee Pottery cabbage leaf ware, *below left*, circa 1890, impressed W in sunburst mark, diameter of saucer 5¾". The Wannopee factory specialized in cabbage leaf ware, which was made from its inception in 1887 into the early twentieth century. The concept was derived from Continental faience of a type made in Italy, Portugal, Germany, and France in the late eighteenth century (Figure 301). *Collection of Dr. & Mrs. Howard Silby*

Figure 301. Italian *maiolica* cabbage leaf plate, *above*, circa 1770. Ware of this type inspired the products of the Wannopee Pottery. Some eighteenth-century Italian *maiolica* was marked with a sun in splendor, from which the company copied its early trademark. *Collection of Dr. & Mrs. Howard Silby*

**M**ottahedeh Founded in 1924, Mottahedeh special-izes in authentic re-production of ceram-ics and metal ware and has frequently copied well-known items, usually those of eighteenth-century origin in United States and European museum col-lections (see Figure 308). A small range of majol-ica reproductions was introduced in 1987, inspired by Victorian originals viewed in London by Mrs. Mildred Mottahedeh, the company's president. About fifteen majolica pieces are now produced exclusively for Mottahedeh in Italy, after designs by George Jones (see Figure 309), Wedgwood, and Joseph Holdcroft. Most pieces bear printed marks including the name Mottahedeh and "Mu-seum Reproduction," but some examples do not bear permanent marks.

Figure 309. Mottahedeh majolica teapot, *above right*, after a George Jones design in the permanent collection of the Smithsonian Institu-tion, height 7″. Including a plate, this model is one of two Motta-hedeh designs after George Jones's popular "Apple Blossom" pattern (see Figures 196 and 309). The company makes a range of more than thirty-five authentic English majolica reproductions. *Mottahedeh Collection*

Figure 310. George Jones majolica teacup and saucer, *right*, in the "Apple Blossom" pattern, circa 1882, diameter of saucer 5″. A typical example of George Jones's "useful" ware in the company's favorite design, now reproduced by Mottahedeh. Teacups were offered for sale in conventional tea sets, in *déjeuner* sets (two cups and saucers, teapot, sugar, creamer, and, usually, a tray), and *solitaire* sets, (only one cup and saucer and a smaller pot). *Collection of Mr. & Mrs. G. Leberfeld*

Figure 311. "Wheel" plates in two sizes, Mottahedeh majolica after designs by George Jones, diameters 8½" and 11¼". *Mottahedeh Collection*

The Haldon Group

An American corporation based in Texas, with showrooms and representatives in many cities, The Haldon Group introduced majolica wares into its established range of decorative earthenware tablewares in 1985. Haldon is the largest distributor in the United States of modern majolica, all of which is manufactured at potteries in Japan. The line has grown from a selection of green-glazed tableware to include a wide range of historic reproductions (Figures 311–314) derived from English and Continental patterns as well as a large selection of pieces designed exclusively for the modern home; of these, some incorporate historic motifs. Majolica sold through The Haldon Group is marked with an ink stamp, and some pieces include the pattern name and date of introduction.

Figure 312. Majolica "Gray Rabbit" covered sauce tureen and spoon by Haldon, circa 1986. The form of this model is derived from a George Jones tureen design of the 1870s. *The Haldon Group Collection*

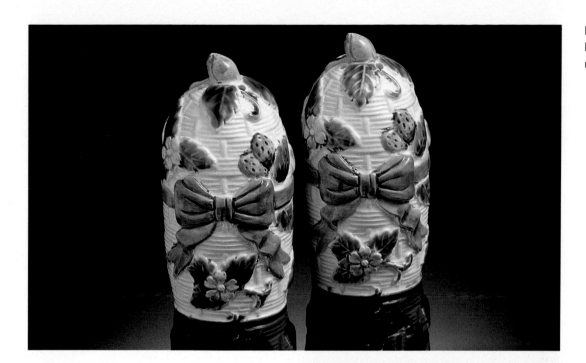

Figure 313. Majolica salt and pepper shakers, *left*, by Haldon, circa 1987. In this model, the familiar ribbon and bow ornament of English Victorian majolica is combined with a modern form. *The Haldon Group Collection*

Figure 314. Majolica sideplate and mug, *right*, in the "Rose" pattern by Haldon, circa 1986. The "Rose" pattern is among the most popular of Haldon's designs. The coffee mug is a good example of contemporary form decorated with Victorian inspiration. *The Haldon Group Collection*

Porta

Established in 1984 by the Portuguese Trade Commission to encourage U.S. trade, Porta has expanded considerably in the last three years, since it began operating independently. Based in New Jersey, with showrooms in New York City, Dallas, and Atlanta, the company imports a wide range of ceramics and some metal ware, all made in Portugal. Most of Porta's majolica range is made by the company established over a century ago by Rafael Bordalo Pinheiro (see chapter 5), which still operates under the family name. Majolica available through Porta, some of which is made exclusively for them, includes tableware in Victorian taste, copied from original examples or made from the Bordalo Pinheiro's factory's collection of old molds, as well as elaborate Victorian reproductions of tureens, Portuguese cabbage leaf ware, articles of modern design, and decorative tiles (Figures 315, 316, and 317). Most examples are marked with the manufacturer's ink stamp, usually a roundel with the name "Bordalo Pinheiro Lda" bordering a frog.

Figure 315. Group of monochrome "majolica"-glazed tableware in the "Flores" pattern, produced by Bordalo Pinheiro for Porta from Victorian originals, 1988. *Porta*

Figure 316. Majolica sauce boat patterned with asparagus by Bordalo Pinheiro for Porta, 1989. *Porta*

Figure 317. Group of four Art Nouveau majolica wall tiles designed by Rafael Bordalo Pinheiro, circa 1900, and made at the modern works, each 5″ × 5″. *Porta*

N o t e s

Archival Reference Abbreviations

MA: Minton Museum Archives, Royal Doulton Tableware Ltd., Stoke-on-Trent, Staffordshire, England.

WA: Wedgwood Archives, Keele University, Keele, Staffordshire, England.

Introduction

1. MA1-45-47: Letter from Henry Cole to Herbert Minton the younger, January 23, 1879. "I recollect asking [Herbert Minton] in the Paris Exhibition of 1849 if the British Exhibition of 1851 should be National or International. . . . He instantly said 'International,' and so it was, and his opinion was the link in the chain. . . . Prince Albert at that time adopted the same idea and brought it about by his influence."

2. Stuart, Denis, ed.: *People of the Potteries.* Keele Staffordshire: Keele University Press, 1985, p. 154.

3. MA1-70 May 14, 1851: Letter from Colin M. Campbell to his mother.

4. Ref: "Summerly's Art Manufacturers," appendix.

5. *Catalog of the International Exhibition,* 1851, Art Journal, p. 44: MA-1380.

6. At the École Centrale des Arts et Manufactures in Paris.

7. Notably, A. Darcel's *Notice des Fayences Peintes Italiennes,* published in 1864, C. Delange's *Recueil de Faiences Italiennes des XVe, XVIe et XVIIe Siècles*; published 1867–1869, and C.D.E. Forthum's *Descriptive Catalogue of the Maiolica, Hispano-Moresque, Persian, Damascus and Rhodian Wares in the South Kensington Museum,* published in 1873.

8. The Soulages Collection of Rennaissance bronzes and ceramics was acquired for the nation and installed in the South Kensington Museum, partly upon the advice of Herbert Minton.

9. A form of earthenware with encaustic decoration, made under Leon Arnoux's direction as an authentic reproduction of ware made at St. Porchaire in France in the sixteenth century. Henri Deux ware was first shown by Minton in 1862 and enjoyed limited success due to extremely high production costs.

10. MA1-1234.

11. Although Luca della Robbia is the best-known exponent of this ware and did make many ceramic innovations to produce it commercially, the fundamentals of his process were known in the Near East as early as the tenth century.

1: English Majolica

1. Atterbury, Paul, & Louise Irvine: *The Doulton Story.* London: The Victoria & Albert Museum, 1980.

2. WA-14193-15: Designs for Buckminster Park, 1886.

3. Ricardo, Halsey: "Of Color in the Architecture of Cities." *Art & Life & The Building & Decoration of Cities,* London, 1897.

4. Austwick, J. and B.: *The Decorated Tile.* London: Pitman House, 1980, p. 54.

5. Austwick, J. and B.: *op. cit.,* p. 61.

6. Austwick, J. and B.: *op cit.,* p. 60.

7. Austwick, J. and B.: *op. cit.,* p. 86.

8. Between 1892 and 1894, over half a million plain white tiles manufactured by T. & R. Boote were used in the construction of one tunnel [the Blackwall] under the Thames in London.

9. Notably, Pierre Emile Jeannest, who taught there for several years following his appointment at Minton's, and Albert Ernest Carrier de Belleuse, who served as Modeling Instructor at the Stoke and Hanley Schools of Art between 1852 and 1855.

10. MA1-31: Wyatt, Digby M., "On the Influence Exercised on Ceramic Manufacturers by the Late Mr. Herbert Minton." *Journal of the Society of Arts,* May 28, 1858, p. 9.

11. *The Art Union of London Annual Journal,* 1848, p. 136.

12. *Ibid.*

13. Hunt, Robert: "Effects of the European Revolutions on British Industry & Art." *The Art Union of London Annual Journal,* 1848, p. 146. "The amount of production stopped in France is perfectly astounding. . .the number of vessels clearing French and German ports from the United States this year will not be one half of the average of the 5 years past. This deficiency in Continental production Britain can and will supply."

14. Fleming, John, and Hugh Honour: *Dictionary of the Decorative Arts.* New York: Harper and Row, 1977, p. 151.

15. Ref: Wyatt, Digby M.: "After the troubles of 1848 in France, Mr. Herbert Minton was so fortunate as to secure the cooperation and services of Leon Arnoux." From an extended obituary of Herbert Minton, *Journal of the Society of Arts,* May 28, 1858. Arnoux's emigration may also have been prompted by financial troubles at his family's pottery in Toulouse, which went into liquidation in 1849; Ref: MA1-618, p. 5.

2: English Majolica and the Evolution of Style

1. *Art Union of London Annual Journal,* 1848, p. 12.

2. His third and final book, "*The True Principles of Pointed or Christian Architecture,*" published in 1841, included his mature views on furniture, decoration, and architecture, and influenced William Morris and John Ruskin.

3. Jacob-Ignaz Hittorff, a Swiss architect and archaeologist, published a number of illustrated works on the architecture of the ancient world in the 1820s and 1830s.

4. These are the only two Egyptian designs by George Jones that are recorded.

5. Hunt, Robert: *Art Union of London Annual Journal,* 1848, p. 221.

6. Jahn's specialities were *Lepidoptera* (butterflies and moths) and *Coleoptera* (beetles and certain weevils). In later life, he was curator of the Hanley Museum.

7. Henderson, Mary F.: *Practical Cooking and Dinner Giving,* 1879.

8. An ornamental version of Gothic Revivalism of Continental taste, typically including figures.

9. As published in Owen Jones's *The Grammar of Ornament,* 1856.

10. Evidence of this still exists in the Minton archives, where several volumes include Arnoux's signature on the plate.

11. MA-(XVI) 1630.

12. Allom, Thomas, and Clemont Pelle: *L'Empire Chinois Illustré,* Fisher Fils et Cie, Paris (undated), circa 1845.

13. Initially in Charles Locke Eastlake's *Hints on Household Taste in Furniture, Upholstery, and Other Details,* London, 1868; U.S. edition, 1872.

14. *In Pursuit of Beauty,* published by the Metropolitan Museum of Arts, Rizzoli, New York, 1986.

15. MA-1713: Dr. Dresser is recorded in Minton's majolica design log book as the supplier of twenty-two design drawings for a variety of ware to be numbered G83 to G104 (circa 1865).

3: The Making of Majolica

1. MA1-1428.

2. MA1-1428.

3. Examples of which were shown at the Great Exhi-

bition and judged to be "fully equal to . . . and considerably cheaper than . . . the German [Dresden] product."

4. MA1-1428.

5. Many samples and raw materials from this Victorian company are preserved in the Gladstone Pottery Museum at Longton, Staffordshire.

6. WA-21614–29.

7. WA-21623–29.

8. MA1-31: Wyatt, Digby M.: "On the influence exercised on Ceramic Manufacturers by the late Mr. Herbert Minton." *Journal of the Society of Arts*, May 28, 1858.

9. WA-21609-29: Letter to Godfrey Wedgwood from Michael Daintry Hollins, dated May 22, 1862. "From our first introduction of . . . majolica . . . we have always charged them at the Parian price and the sale has been quite to our satisfaction."

10. Becker, Bernard H.: "China Making at Stoke-on-Trent." *The English Illustrated Magazine*, London, Mac-Millan, 1885.

11. MA1: Minton's Art Library in 1871 comprised over 200 illustrated books, many of which were acquired at considerable expense.

12. Lamb, Andrew: "The Press and Labour's Response to Pottery-making Machinery in the Northern Staffordshire Pottery Industry." *Journal of Ceramic History*, Stoke-on-Trent City Museums, No. 9, 1977.

13. "Majolica Vases, Patent Wall Tiles and Mosaics by Herbert Minton and Co." *The Illustrated London News*, June 1851.

14. Becker, Bernard H.: "*China Making at Stoke-on-Trent*," *The English Illustrated Magazine*, London, (MacMillan), 1885.

4: English Majolica Manufacturers and Their Marks

1. Wedgwood, Josiah C.: *Staffordshire Pottery and Its History*, New York: publisher unknown, 1947.

2. Arnoux's role at Minton was not limited to the conventional duties of an art director. According to an extended obituary in *The Staffordshire Advertiser*, September 6, 1902, his title was a rather inappropriate one: ". . . to superintend the artistic department was the minor part of his daily duties. . . . There was not a branch in the complicated run of manufacture. . . . that escaped his vigilant supervision."

3. MA1-1234: Which began with G1, design for a vase in majolica copied from an example in the South Kensington Museum in the summer of 1849.

4. MA1-1234.

5. MA1-1234: No majolica was shown at the London Exhibition of 1849.

6. "Majolica vases, patent wall tiles and mosaics by Herbert Minton & Company." *The Illustrated London News*, June 1851.

7. MA1-17: letter from Colin Minton Campbell to his mother, May 14, 1851.

8. MA1-17.

9. MA1-17.

10. MA1-17.

11. MA1-17.

12. Wyatt, Digby M.: *op. cit.*, p. 9. Herbert Minton commenting on the Great Exhibition of 1851.

13. Albert Carrier was artistic director of the Sèvres Porcelain Factory from 1875 until his death in 1887.

14. Fleming, John and Hugh Honour: *Dictionary of the Decorative Arts*. New York: Harper and Row, 1977, pp. 151–152. Albert Carrier also obtained celebrity as the employer of the young Auguste Rodin (from 1864).

15. MA1-1576.

16. WA-29057/2-44.

17. *The London Evening Standard*, May 19, 1862.

18. *The Art Union of London Journal*, March 1868, p. 59.

19. *Ibid.*

20. MA1-1380: Such pieces were typically stored or owned by Minton agents, including Thomas Goode and Co., of London, who have represented Minton for over a century, and, in the early majolica period, Phillips of Oxford Street.

21. MA1-48.

22. MA1-43-44: 1,517 employees were counted in 1876, in Stoke-on-Trent and London, including 207 enamelers at the earthenware works.

23. MA1-1277: Annual costs for models and molds used in earthenware production were estimated to be one half of those for raw materials in the 1870s.

24. MA1-231: Turnover records/profit and loss, 1885–1900.

25. MA1-1380.

26. On Wednesday, January 29, 1902, at one o'clock precisely.

27. In 1844, a large portion of the Wedgwood holdings were sold off as the company neared bankruptcy. The Etruria works itself was offered at auction but failed to meet the reserve.

28. Meteyard, Eliza: *The Wedgwood Handbook*, Staffordshire: publisher unknown, 1875.

29. WA-21609-29: letter to Michael Daintry Hollins dated May 22, 1862.

30. *Catalog of Majolica Fancy Articles, February 1880*. Wedgwood Museum Archives, Barlaston.

31. WA-28000A-38.

32. WA-28000A-38.

33. Batkin, Maureen: *Wedgwood Ceramics 1846–1959*. London: Richard Dennis, 1982.

34. Over 2,500 examples.

35. In the 1870s, Wedgwood offered over twenty distinct varieties of ornamental ware.

36. George Jones Archives, Wedgwood Museum at Barlaston.

37. MA1-173: George Jones is listed as an apprentice in 1850 and had left Minton's employ by 1859.

38. "Asia" was represented by camels; "Africa" by a pair of lions; "America" by buffalo and "Europe" by a pair of deer with rabbits.

39. George Jones Archives, Wedgwood Museum at Barlaston.

40. George Jones Archives, Wedgwood Museum at Barlaston.

41. George Jones Archives, Wedgwood Museum at Barlaston.

42. The earliest number recorded by the author is actually 627, for the "Harvest" pattern bread tray, which is molded with the motto "CUT AND COME AGAIN" against sheaves of wheat.

43. Not to be confused with the Sutherland Pottery in Normacott Road, Longton, operated in the 1870s by Messrs. Skelson and Plant, porcelain manufacturers.

44. Jewitt, Llewellyn: *Ceramic Art of Great Britain, 1878*. New York: reprinted by Arco Publishing, 1971, p.101.

45. Stuart, Denis, ed.: *People of the Potteries*. Keele University Press, 1985, p. 96.

46. Jewitt, Llewellyn: *Ceramic Art of Great Britain, 1878.* New York: reprinted by Arco Publishing, 1971, p.135.

47. Stuart, Denis, ed.: *People of the Potteries*. Keele University Press, 1985, p. 96.

48. Godden, Geoffrey: "Victorian Ceramic Artists." *Apollo*, March 1959, p. 76.

49. "Biography of W. B. Moore." Hanley Reference Library, July 1899, Vol. 4, p.187.

50. "Description of Brown-Westhead, Moore's Cauldon Works." *Farmer's New Borough Almanac*, G. E. Farmer, publisher,1885.

51. Ibid.

52. "Biography of W. B. Moore." Hanley Reference Library, July 1899, Vol. 4, p.187.

53. According to Leon Arnoux, as quoted in *The Illustrated London News*, June 5, 1852.

54. Godden, Geoffrey: *Handbook of British Pottery and Porcelain Marks*. London: Barrie and Jenkins, 1968.

5: Majolica in Continental Europe

1. Haslam, Michael: "Bernard Palissy." *Connoisseur*, September 1975, pp. 12–17.

2. The Sauvageot Collection, including many Palissy-inspired ceramics of the sixteenth century, was installed in the Louvre Museum in Paris in 1856.

3. Ref: MA-993, MA-1025, MA-1035.

4. Ref: Fleming, John, and Hugh Honouri *Dictionary of the Decorative Arts*. New York: Harper and Row, 1977.

5. Ref: MA-1380.

6: Majolica in America

1. *The Congressional Record*, March 2, 1861; c. 68, Section 17, Part 2, 12 Stat., 178. Under this statute, majolica-type ware was subject to an import tariff of 25 percent.

2. This term is used in *Masterpieces of the Centennial Exhibition*, published by Gebbie and Barrie, Philadelphia, 1876, Vol. III, p. CLXXIX.

3. Varick, Vernon: "Notes on Early New Jersey Pottery." *Hobbies*, July 1944, p. 64.

4. *New Jersey Potteries 1685–1876*. Newark: The Newark Museum Association, 1914, p.18.

5. Ref: *The Crockery Journal*, Vol. 1, No. 5, January 23, 1875, pp. 4–5. For a full discussion, refer to Stradling, J.G.: "American Ceramics and the Philadelphia Centennial." *Antiques* magazine, July 1976, pp.146–158.

6. Berrill, M. Jacquelyn: "Glass & China, The Past in My Hands." *Hobbies*, January 1948, p. 68.

7. Memorial Hall is a notable exception.

8. The exact figure was 10,164,489, according to Gebbie and Barrie, in *Masterpieces of the Centennial Exhibition*, 1876, Vol. III, p. CLXXXVI.

9. Gebbie and Barrie, Publishers: *Masterpieces of the Centennial Exhibition*, 1876, Vol. III, p. CLXXX.

10. Gebbie and Barrie, Publishers: *Masterpieces of the Centennial Exhibition*, 1876, Vol. III, p. CLXXVII.

11. According to Fryatt, F.E., in *Harper's* magazine, February 1881, as quoted by Schwartz, Marvin D., in "Fine American Ceramics of the Victorian Period." *Antiques* magazine, April 1960, p. 389.

12. The date 1882 is suggested by Arthur B. James in *The Potters and Potteries of Chester County, Pennsylvania*, 1945. The date 1879 is given by Ruth Irwin Weidner, *op cit*.

13. Berrill, Jacquelyn M.: "Glass and China: The Past in My Hands." *Hobbies*, January 1948, p. 64.

14. In the 1870s, railroad building was highly important to the Pennsylvania iron industry, including the Griffen family. Between 1876 and 1880, many employees of the Phoenixville Pottery moved to Pittsburgh for the purpose of railway building, causing the kilns to be shut down for much of that time.

15. This number is suggested by Ruth Irwin Weidner in "The Majolica Wares of Griffen Smith & Company." (*Spinning Wheel*, January–February 1980, pp.13–17). It is more likely that about 200 were employed.

16. Berrill, Jacquelyn M.: "Glass and China: The Past in My Hands." *Hobbies*, January 1948, p. 65.

17. Five bottle ovens operated at the Phoenixville works, according to Weidner, *op. cit.*, p. 14.

18. Weidner, *op. cit.*, p. 17.

19. Clement, Arthur, W., *Notes on American Ceramics 1607–1743*, Brooklyn Museum Exhibition.

20. Rickerson, Wildey C.: *Majolica: It's Fun to Collect*. Deep River, Connecticut: published privately, 1963.

21. Rickerson, Wildey C.: *Majolica: It's Fun to Collect*. Deep River, Connecticut: published privately, 1963.

22. Evans, Paul: *Art Pottery of the United States*. New York: Charles Scribner's Sons, 1974, pp.100–102.

23. This date is recorded in Wildey C. Rickerson's *Majolica: It's Fun to Collect*.

24. "Awards and Report of the Judges of the Pottery and Porcelain Exhibition." October 16–November 13, 1888. Philadelphia: The Philadelphia Museum and School of Industrial Art, 1888.

25. Ketchum, William: *Potters and Potteries of New York State 1650–1900*, Syracuse, New York: Syracuse University Press, 1987.

26. The other was the New York City Pottery of James Carr.

27. Stradling, J.G.: "American Ceramics and the Philadelphia Centennial." *Antiques*, July 1976, p. 154.

Glossary

Aesthetic style An approach to design and ornamentation practiced in France, Britain, and the United States between circa 1865 and 1885, influenced by principles that emphasized the innovative application of "art" to all areas of decorative art. The ensuing movement was strongly guided by *Japonisme* and contemporary progressive writings on interior design.

Body Any mixture of clays and minerals suitable for ceramic manufacture.

Bottle oven A *kiln* of bottle shape.

Cachepôt Of French origin, a nineteenth-century term for an ornamental flowerpot cover, sometimes made in *majolica*.

Calcareous Composed of or characteristic of calcium carbonate or limestone; chalky. A property of many ceramic bodies, especially those used for the production of *tin-glazed earthenware*.

Calcining Heating a material to a point where some ingredients are burnt away and its physical properties are changed, as in burning to an ash, and allowing it to cool before use. The process is used in the production of plaster of Paris (calcined gypsum).

Continuous kiln Any *kiln* or arrangement of kilns that may be kept firing without the need to cool the entire fabric during unpacking. Example: a tunnel kiln.

Creamware A type of lead-glazed *earthenware* widely made in *The Potteries* during the third quarter of the eighteenth century. Also known as "cream-colored earthenware."

Earthenware A generic term for porous, opaque ceramic bodies; *pottery*.

Email Ombrant A decorating technique patented by Baron du *Tremblay* at the Roubelles porcelain works in France in 1842 and later practiced by Wedgwood. The process involves flooding intaglio impressed designs with translucent, colored glazes to create perspective.

Faience (1) Glazed *terra cotta* as used for architectural ceramics; (2) See *tin-glazed earthenware*.

Glaze A glassy covering on ceramic material, sometimes achieved intrinsically on *porcelain*.

Glost kiln A kiln used exclusively for glaze firing. Other specialized kilns include "biscuit," "enamel" (finishing), and "salt glaze" kilns.

High-temperature colors The palette of colors that, when applied to ceramics, withstand the high temperatures necessary to fuse with *tin glaze*. The palette consists of green, derived from copper oxide; blue, from cobalt; purple, from manganese; yellow, from antimony; and orange, from iron. Also: *Gros Feu* colors.

Japonisme The Japanese influence on western decorative arts, especially the *progressive design* of France and England during the third quarter of the nineteenth century.

Jardiniere A stand or large vessel for holding potted plants; a planter. Very common in formal Victorian interiors and conservatories.

Kiln A furnace or oven made of *refractory* material used for firing ceramics.

Lithophanie A porcelain panel molded in intaglio with a pictorial subject that appears in perspective in transmitted light. Lithophanies were first made in Germany about 1827, and were made at Minton later in the century. *Email Ombrant* uses a variation of the technique.

Maiolica See *tin-glazed earthenware*.

Majolica (1) Tradename given to a family of ornamental *earthenwares* decorated with polychromatic, opaque glazes devised by Leon Arnoux at Minton between 1848 and 1851; Also, Majolica glazes; (2) A variant of the word *maiolica*.

Mignonette box A type of *cache pôt*.

Palissy ware Any ceramics made in the style of Bernard Palissy, including those made by his contemporaries.

Parian A type of *porcelain* resembling the pure white marble, found on Paros, a Greek island in the Aegean Sea, first produced at the Copeland factory in 1844 and used mainly for statuary or figural molded ware; also, *Parian ware*.

Pâte sur pâte An advanced method of decorating *porcelain* by painting on and later carving successive layers of liquid clay (slip), developed at the Sèvres factory in the mid-nineteenth century and later practiced at Minton.

Porcelain A white, resonant, nonporous, and translucent ceramic *body*.

Potteries, the The area of North Staffordshire in England that has been the most active and most influential center of the ceramics industry in Europe for three centuries. Still erroneously referred to as "the Five Towns," the term applies to a conglomeration of six towns—Stoke-on-Trent, Burslem, Fenton, Hanley, Longton, and Tunstall—that for economic reasons attempted to form a federation in the early years of this century. Bordering municipalities include Barlaston, Cobridge, Lane End, and Shelton. Also, Staffordshire Potteries.

Pottery 1. *Earthenware*. 2. Any works designed for the manufacture of ceramics.

Progressive design Any attempt to design using innovative techniques, materials, and principles as opposed to traditionalism; modernism.

Reduction firing The process used to produce iridescent or lustrous glaze effects, as found on *majolica*, by creating an oxygen-depleted atmosphere within the *kiln* at critical stages in the firing.

Refractory Resistant to the effects of high temperatures, as in refractory clay, also called "fire clays."

Second Empire The French political period under Napoleon III, circa 1850 to 1870, when numerous historical styles in decorative art were popularly revived, notably the Louis XVI taste.

Slip A clay in liquid suspension.

Slip casting A common method of reproducing hollow *ware* by pouring *slip* into a hollow plaster mold. After a period, a layer of clay dries and adheres to the mold wall, and the surplus is poured off, leaving a clay vessel that is removed when hardened by disassembling the mold.

Spill vase A vessel, usually cylindrical, to hold spills, *i.e.*, thin strips of wood or twisted paper used for lighting pipes or candles, sometimes made in *majolica*. Spill vases were a common feature on Victorian mantelpieces.

Staffordshire knot A device in the form of a knotted rope, loosely of figure-of-eight shape, sometimes incorporated in the marks of Staffordshire potters.

Terra cotta A type of simple *earthenware*, usually red in color and often containing "grog" (ceramic material which has been previously fired and ground to a powder).

Tin-glazed earthenware *Earthenware* made white by a covering of opaque glaze containing oxides of lead and tin combined with a silicate of potash, the earliest examples of which were made in the Near East in the ninth century; high-quality examples that inspired some Victorian *majolica* were made in Renaissance Italy and Spain. It was widely made for domestic use in eighteenth-century Europe, where it was known under various names, depending on the region of origin, including *Faience* (France and parts of Northern Europe); Delft ware (The Netherlands and Britain); and *Maiolica* (Southern Europe, North Africa, and the Near East).

Tremblay See *Email Ombrant*.

Tube-lining The application of *slip* onto a surface for decorative effect by squeezing it through a nozzle in a similar fashion used to decorate cakes with icing.

Ware Any ceramic material in any state of production—raw, unglazed or finished.

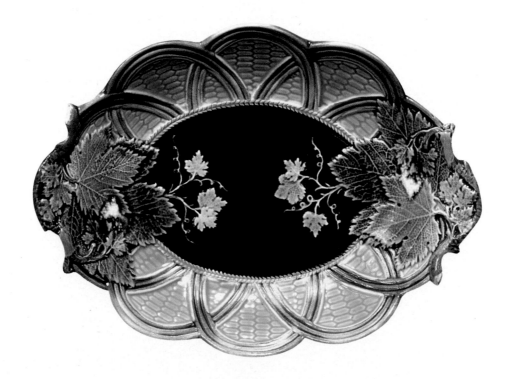

Bibliography

Books on Majolica

Karmason, Marilyn G., with Joan B. Stacke: *Majolica*. New York: Harry N. Abrams, Inc., 1989.

Marks, Mariann K.: *Majolica Pottery*. Collector Books, 1983; Second Series, 1986.

Rickerson, Wildey C.: *Majolica; It's Fun to Collect*. Deep River, Connecticut: privately published, 1963.

Rebert, M. Charles: *American Majolica: 1850–1900*. Des Moines, Iowa: Wallace-Homestead Book Company, 1981.

Exhibition Publications, Trade Catalogs and Reports on Majolica

Aslin, Elizabeth and Paul Atterbury: *Minton 1798–1810*. London: Victoria and Albert Museum, 1976.

Bailey, Joseph T., W.P.P. Longfellow and Henry Steele: *Awards and Report of the Judges, The Pennsylvania Museum and School of Art Pottery and Porcelain Exhibition*. Philadelphia: 1888.

Bonython, Elizabeth: *Art Applied to the Home: The Household Taste of Henry Cole and His Circle*. The Victoria and Albert Album, Vol. III. London: DeMontfort Publishing Ltd., 1984, pp.161–167.

Catalogue of Majolica of Griffen Smith and Co. Reprint of 1884 original. Phoenixville, Pennsylvania: Brooke Weidner, 1960.

Catalogue of Principal Works Exhibited at the International Exhibition. Newcastle-under-Lyme: B. Dilworth, 1862, pp.12–16. Minton Archives, MA1-1380.

Cecil, Victoria: *Minton "Majolica."* Exhibition catalog for Jeremy Cooper Ltd.; London: Trefoil Books Ltd., 1982.

English Ceramic Circle, ed.: *English Pottery and Porcelain Catalog of 1943*. London: Routledge and Kegan Paul Ltd., 1949.

The Jackfield Decorative Tile Industry. Brochure. Ironbridge, Ironbridge Gorge Museum Trust, 1978.

King, Jean Callan: *English Majolica*. New York: Report from The Twenty-Seventh Wedgwood International Seminar, April 21–24, 1982.

The Masterpieces of the Centennial International Exhibition. Vols. I, II, and III. Philadelphia: 1876.

Victoriana: An Exhibition of the Arts of the Victorian Era in America. New York: The Brooklyn Museum, April 7– June 5, 1960.

Works of General Reference, British Ceramics

Atterbury, Paul, and Louise Irvine: *The Doulton Story*. London: The Victoria and Albert Museum, 1980.

Batkin, Maureen: *Wedgwood Ceramics 1846–1959*. London: Richard Dennis, 1982.

Bemrose, Geoffrey: *Nineteenth Century English Pottery and Porcelain*. London: Faber and Faber, 1952.

Godden, Geoffrey: *An Illustrated Encyclopedia of British Pottery and Porcelain*. Second edition. London: Barrie and Jenkins, 1980.

Godden, Geoffrey: *Handbook of British Pottery and Porcelain Marks*. London: Barrie and Jenkins, 1968.

Godden, Geoffrey: *Victorian Porcelain*. New York: T. Nelson and Sons, 1961.

Hughes, Bernard: *Victorian Pottery and Porcelain*. London: Spring Books, 1959.

Jewitt, Llewellyn: *Ceramic Art of Great Britain*, 1878. New York: reprinted by Arco Publishing, 1971.

Pottery and Porcelain in 1876: An Art Student's Ramble Through some of the China Shops of London. London: Field and Tuer, 1877. Minton Archives.

Stuart, Denis, ed.: *People of the Potteries*. Volume I. Staffordshire: Keele University Department of Adult Education, 1985.

Works of General Reference, American Ceramics

Barber, Edwin Atlee: *Handbooks of the Philadelphia Museum*. Philadelphia: Philadelphia Museum, 1906.

Barber, Edwin Atlee: *Marks of American Potters*. Philadelphia: Patterson and White, 1904.

Barber, Edwin Atlee: *The Pottery and Porcelain of the United States*. New York: G. P. Putnam's Sons, 1893.

Cameron, Elizabeth: *Encyclopedia of Pottery and Porcelain, 1800–1960*. New York: Facts-on-File Publications, 1986.

Clark, Garth: *A Century of Ceramics in the United States 1878–1978*. New York: E. P. Dutton, 1978.

Clement, Arthur: *Notes on American Ceramics 1607– 1943*. New York: Brooklyn Museum, undated.

Evans, Paul: *Art Pottery of the United States*. New York: Charles Scribner's Sons, 1974.

James, Arthur B.: *The Potters and Potteries of Chester County, Pennsylvania*. Exton, Pennsylvania: reprinted by Schiffer Publishers Ltd., 1978.

Ketchum, William C. Jr.: *Early Potters and Potteries of New York State*. New York: Funk and Wagnall's, 1970.

New Jersey Potteries 1685–1876. Newark: The Newark Museum Association, 1914.

Spargo, John: *Early American Pottery and China*. New York: The Century Company, 1926.

Watkins, Lura Woodside: *Early New England Potters and Their Wares*. Cambridge: The Harvard University Press, 1950.

Additional Works of General Reference

Austwick, J. and B.: *The Decorated Tile*. London: Pitman House, 1980.

Curl, James Stevens: *Victorian Architecture*. London: David and Charles, Ltd., 1973.

Jones, Owen: *The Grammar of Ornament*. London: Messrs. Day and Son, 1856; reprinted by Studio Editions, 1987.

Lockett, Terence A.: *Collecting Victorian Tiles*. London: The Antique Collectors Club, 1979.

Stern, Anna, in *Encyclopedia of Collectibles* ("Majolica: Flamboyant Victorian Ware.") New York: Time-Life Books, 1979.

Articles in Periodicals and Journals: Antiques

Rolfe, Richard C.: "Introducing. . ." January 1943.

Rolfe, Richard C.: "The Glass and China Cupboard." February 1943, pp. 82–83.

Schwartz, Marvin D.: "Fine American Ceramics of the Victorian Period." April 1960, pp. 386–389.

Stradling, J.G.: "American Ceramics and the Philadelphia Centennial." July 1976.

Watkins, Lura Woodside; "Colorful Ceramics of the 1880s in a Family Collection." January 1968, pp. 100–103.

Apollo

Godden, Geoffrey: "Artists at Minton's." December 1962, pp. 797–798.

Godden, Geoffrey: "Thomas Kirkby: Victorian Ceramic Artist." September 1960, pp. 63–66.

Godden, Geoffrey: "Victorian Ceramic Artists—I." (Antonin Boullemier) March 1959, p. 76.

Godden, Geoffrey: "Victorian Ceramic Artists—IV." (Thomas Allen) August 1959, p. 29.

Godden, Geoffrey: "Victorian Ceramic Artists—V." (Charles Toft) September 1959, p. 51.

Connoisseur

"American Ceramic Types and Their European Background." December 1944, pp. 115–119.

Atterbury, Paul: "Minton Majolica." August 1976, pp. 304–308.

Haslam, Michael: "Bernard Palissy." September 1975, pp. 12–17.

Wilson, Lisbet: "Down from the Attic." February 1984, pp. 68–72.

Hobbies

Berrill, M. Jacquelyn: "The Past in My Hands." January 1948, pp. 64–68.

"The Enigma of Majolica." May 1949, pp. 111–115.

Freeman, Larry: "A Corn King's Hobby." April 1950, pp. 77, 80.

Varick, Vernon: "Notes on Early New Jersey Pottery." July 1944, p. 64.

House and Garden

Greene, Elaine: "Majolica." September 1983, pp. 100–101.

Holden, M.: "Early American Household Pottery." April 1921, pp. 30–31, 74–78.

Lerrick, Joan: *Majolica Mania*." September 1982, pp. 83–84, 136–137.

Miscellaneous Periodicals

Adams, John: "Potters Parade." *Pottery and Glass*, February and March 1951. Minton Archives.

Anderton, Paul: "A Trade Union Year: 1864, an extract from the Transactions of the Executive Committee for the Hollow Ware Pressers Union." *Journal of Ceramic History*, Stoke-on-Trent City Museums, No. 9, 1977, pp. 9–32.

The Art Journal of London, 1849, pp. 299–300. Minton Archives, MA1-E1.

The Art Journal of London, 1853, pp. 13–14. Minton Archives, MA1-E1.

The Art Journal of London, 1856. Minton Archives, MA1-E1.

The Art-Union Monthly Journal of the Arts, Chapman and Hall, London, Volume X, 1848.

Barber, Edwin Atlee: "Recent Advances in the Pottery Industry." *The Popular Science Monthly*, January 1892, pp. 289–306.

Becker, Bernard H.: "China Making at Stoke-on-Trent." *The English Illustrated Magazine*, MacMillan, London, 1885.

Elliott, Gordon: "Nineteenth Century Staffordshire." *Ceramic Monthly*, March 1977, pp. 29–36.

"Griffen, Smith and Hill Co." *National Antiques Review*, October 1971.

King, Jean Callan: "Majolica—A Pottery for Everyone." *House Beautiful*, February 1985, pp. 63–65, 118.

Lamb, Andrew: "The Press and Labour's Response to Pottery-Making Machinery in the North Staffordshire Pottery Industry." *Journal of Ceramic Industry*, Stoke-on-Trent City Museums, No. 9, 1977, pp. 1–8.

The Late Mr. Colin Minton Campbell." *The Building News*, February 12, 1885, p. 241. Minton Archives, MA1/1234.

"The Late Mr. Leon Arnoux, of Stoke-on-Trent: A Biographical Sketch." *The Staffordshire Advertiser*, September 6, 1902, pp. 3–12. Minton Archives.

"Majolica Vases, Patent Wall Tiles, and Mosaics by Herbert Minton and Co." *The Illustrated London News*, June 1851. Minton Archives.

"Pottery Veterans—4: The Man Who Packed an Elephant." *Pottery Gazette*, April, 1949, p. 373. Minton Archives.

Ricardo, Halsey: "Of Color in the Architecture of Cities." *Art and Life and the Decoration of Cities*, 2897.

Weidner, Ruth Irwin: "The Majolica Wares of Griffen Smith and Co." *Spinning Wheel*, January 1980.

Wyatt, M. Digby: "On the Influence Exercised on Ceramic Manufacturers by the Late Mr. Herbert Minton." *Journal of the Society of Arts*, May 28, 1858, pp. 1–11. Minton Archives, MA-31.

Index